# DREAMSMEN

## THE FINAL COMBAT

### RACHEL S. SENIOR

CLAY BRIDGES
PRESS

**Dreamsmen**
The Final Combat

Copyright © 2020 by Rachel S. Senior

Published by Clay Bridges in Houston, TX
www.ClayBridgesPress.com

Scripture quotations are taken from the Holy Bible, New International Version®, NIV®. Copyright © 1973, 1978, 1984, 2011 by Biblica, Inc.™ Used by permission of Zondervan. All rights reserved worldwide. www.zondervan.com The "NIV" and "New International Version" are trademarks registered in the United States Patent and Trademark Office by Biblica, Inc.™

ISBN: 978-1-953300-00-3
eISBN: 978-1-953300-06-5

Special Sales: Clay Bridges titles are available in wholesale quantity. Please visit www.claybridgesbulk.com to order 10 or more copies at a retail discount. Custom imprinting or excerpting can also be done to fit special needs. Contact Clay Bridges at Info@ClayBridgesPress.com.

# TABLE OF CONTENTS

# ACKNOWLEDGMENTS

I want to acknowledge my Kingdom Empowerment Center Church family who not only encouraged the Dreamer in me but also pushed me to step out and teach the power of the Dream. Your support and faith in what God has given me to give to the world means more to me than you can ever imagine.

I also want to acknowledge Prophet Brenda Culpepper who six years ago, in her renown "School of the Prophets" class saw the "Seer" in me, activated the "Dreamer" in me, and helped me to understand the nature of the gifting that was within me.

Finally, I would like to acknowledge and thank my children, Aj, Zoe, Reya, Christian, Mikey, and Nessie, for understanding the time Mommy had to sacrifice from you to complete the assignment God had given me in the form of a book. Thank you. Mommy loves you.

A very special thanks to my mother, Elder Sandy Sewell, who provided me deep insight and firsthand knowledge to support the message of the book. I also want to offer her a special thanks for taking the time to read through the manuscript while offering her editing support as needed.

Finally, I want to thank my husband, Pastor Michael Senior. Without your support, this book could not have been possible. Thank you for your input, your faith, your encouragement, and the physical support you put in taking care of family needs and home, allowing me the quiet time to complete this divine work. I am forever grateful to you, Angel Baby!

# DREAMSMEN

*With Power to See*

# CHAPTER ONE

# FICTION OR HARSH REALITY

*T*he *Avengers, X-Men, Transformers:* In my opinion these are all superhero movie classics that people all over the world enjoy. They have all the makings of what an amazing superhero story entails. That is, they all have villains or situations that can't be defeated or overcome with a nation's average militia, government forces, or public safety agencies, no matter how well trained or elite they may be. The audience can bank on seeing some incredible strength, power, agility, speed, ridiculous skills, or superhuman gifts executed by characters who go far beyond the limits of the average human. People are saved, lives are spared, evil plots are annihilated, and potential threats are completely buried—all at the hands of some incredibly powerful superheroes.

But what makes them super? They all possess a power or specific gift that exceeds the natural laws of physics for humans. In other words, they have the ability to do something no ordinary human can. The Avengers possess superhuman powers that make them a powerful group of soldiers who become great defenders and protectors of Earth. They have the power to fly, manipulate weather and energy, heal quickly, and recover from injuries that would be fatal for the average person. They possess incredible strength, speed, agility, and more. The

X-Men can read minds, freeze things, extract power from others, walk through walls, manipulate the weather, and more. Then there are the Transformers whose very makeup and design exceed all things human. They are literally warrior robot giants made and trained for war.

I could go on and on about the powers, strengths, abilities, and how the very use of them in every superhero movie helped earth reach a happy ending, but there is something about each one of these tales that I find much more worthy of attention. All three superhero movies share a very similar and disheartening fate—a fate that is unfavorable toward the very characters once considered to be "superheroes."

Despite all the people that were saved, all the fights that were won, all the villains that were apprehended or taken down, and despite the fact that these heroes were earth's greatest defenders, at some point, the governments they had defended began to see the heroes as a threat to mankind. Yes, that's right! In the end, these superheroes' hardest fight became the fight that unexpectantly arose between them and the governmental powers they had protected. In *Captain America: Civil War*, it was the secretary of state who sat the Avengers down to tell them that their powers had made them arrogant, reckless, and unconcerned that their abilities were causing fear, casualties, and discomfort among the people. Consequently, they were given an ultimatum to intervene only at the request of the government even if the danger posed extended far beyond the government's ability to respond appropriately. Should they choose to do otherwise, they were told that they would be prosecuted like common criminals; this threat forced a number of the heroes into hiding.

In *Transformers*, the Autobots saw the same fate. They had stood side by side in battle with US Special Government Forces for years, but when the US felt that the Autobots' very existence threatened their power, they turned on them hoping to build a better brand or model that could be controlled. This sent many of the once-acclaimed hero Autobots into hiding.

In *X-Men*, the mere fact that they (being the mutants) had such unique abilities put them at war with the government from the very beginning. The government feared the X-Men's gifts, what they could expose, and what they could do if their gifts were left unchecked. Therefore, the government searched for a way to control how and when the gifted mutants were used. If that could not be done, then the next plan of action was to stop the very operation of their gifts by any means necessary.

Different movies, same endings. At some point the very gifts and powers exhibited by these heroes sparked fear in the governmental authorities. Suddenly, superhero allies became governmental adversaries simply because the governmental powers felt challenged by what the heroes could do. While the heroes were carrying out their purposes, the government started taking notes and jotting down questions: "Would their gifts outshine our position of authority? Would we lose control? Would people begin to look to them? Could they start ordering us around? Would we lose our position of power?" Ultimately, the superheroes' gifts caused the governmental powers to feel inadequate and insecure among their people even though these heroes only used their super abilities for good. So, in an effort to maintain a position of control, and to prove to the heroes that they did not have "the power," these heroes were made to be seen as enemies of the state for exercising the very purpose of their gifts.

Hey, but this is all just the movies, right? No way would leaders make enemies out of people who are working to save lives and give people their best chance at life. No way would leaders wage war on people who are only using their power for good because it appears to threaten the leaders' power. Is this twist merely fiction, or is this an all-too-common reality frequently seen and experienced in our world today?

Okay, so maybe we don't have men and women running around in suits with abnormal strength, speed, or power to manipulate objects or weather. Maybe there is no hostile government takeover that has men and women with special powers in hiding—concealing who they are and what they can do. But this scenario is not very far off from what took place hundreds and hundreds of years ago. Nor is it any different from a very real phenomenon happening in the church today.

A superhero is defined by the *Merriam-Webster* dictionary as "an exceptionally skillful or successful person" and "a fictional hero having extraordinary or superhuman powers." By those two definitions alone, the Bible is filled with superheroes. Biblical superheroes are by no means fictional, but they do possess the capability or supernatural skill to overtake something or someone whose power or abilities are much too threatening for the average person operating at his best to oppose. Perhaps the average man lacks the super-strength, ability, power, or faith necessary to conquer the opposing villain, but the superhero chosen for the job of bringing the villain down or turning the situation around is supernaturally equipped to succeed in doing the job.

Do you recall the very famous Bible story of David and Goliath? Here David is depicted as the superhero, and Goliath is the giant villain. According to the text, Goliath had the whole land in fear. He was taunting the people, hovering over them like a terrible plague, and no army or man would dare to stand up to him.

> *Goliath stood and shouted to the ranks of Israel, "Why do you come out and line up for battle? Am I not a Philistine, and are you not the servants of Saul? Choose a man and have him come down to me. If he is able to fight and kill me, we will become your subjects; but if I overcome him and kill him, you will become our subjects and serve us." Then the Philistine said, "This day I defy the armies of Israel! Give me a man and let us fight each other." On hearing the Philistine's words, Saul and all the Israelites were dismayed and terrified.*
>
> —1 Sam. 17:8–11

> *For forty days the Philistine came forward every morning and evening and took his stand.*
>
> —1 Sam. 17:16

*Whenever the Israelites saw the man, they all fled from him in great fear.*

—1 Sam. 17:24

Imagine that an earthly villain comes to attack, conquer, and rule over the land, and the governmental powers stand helpless against him. How fictional is that, really? Yet in a great time of despair God had already established a superhero—one who had a superpower called faith, combined with great warrior skills endowed on him from God Himself. He didn't even use the Israelites' weapons or their armor. He went with the powers and abilities he had to take Goliath down. Of course, as the Bible tells it, with a rock and a sling, he took the giant down, took his sword, and decapitated the body of the giant.

*David said to Saul, "Let no one lose heart on account of this Philistine; your servant will go and fight him." Saul replied, "You are not able to go out against this Philistine and fight him; you are only a young man, and he has been a warrior from his youth." But David said to Saul, "Your servant has been keeping his father's sheep. When a lion or a bear came and carried off a sheep from the flock, I went after it, struck it and rescued the sheep from its mouth. When it turned on me, I seized it by its hair, struck it and killed it. Your servant has killed both the lion and the bear; this uncircumcised Philistine will be like one of them, because he has defied the armies of the living God. The LORD who rescued me from the paw of the lion and the paw of the bear will rescue me from the hand of this Philistine."*

—1 Sam. 17:32–37

*David said to the Philistine, "You come against me with sword and spear and javelin, but I come against you in the name of the LORD Almighty, the God of the armies of Israel, whom you have defied. This day the* LORD *will deliver you into my hands, and I'll strike you down and cut off your head. This very day I will give the carcasses of the Philistine army to the birds and the wild animals, and the whole world will know that there is a God in Israel. All those gathered here will know that it is not by sword or spear that the* LORD *saves; for the battle is the* LORD'*s, and he will give all of you into our hands." As the Philistine moved closer to attack him, David ran quickly toward the battle line to meet him. Reaching into his bag and taking out a stone, he slung it and struck the Philistine on the forehead. The stone sank into his forehead, and he fell facedown on the ground. So David triumphed over the Philistine with a sling and a stone; without a sword in his hand he struck down the Philistine and killed him.*

*—1 Sam. 17:45–50*

The Bible says that the people began to rejoice. The government, the ruling authority, rejoiced and rewarded the superhero David. But just like in *Transformers, The Avengers,* and *X-Men,* the very government David protected began to feel threatened by what David could do.

*When the men were returning home after David had killed the Philistine, the women came out from all the towns of Israel to meet King Saul with singing and dancing, with joyful songs and with timbrels and lyres. As they danced, they sang: "Saul has slain his thousands, and David his tens of thousands." Saul was very angry; this refrain displeased him greatly. "They have credited David with tens of thousands,"* he thought, *"but me with only thousands. What more can he get but the kingdom?" And from that time on Saul kept a close eye on David.*

*—1 Sam. 18:6–9*

Just like that, David became the enemy and was forced into hiding for doing what he was purposed to do. Does this sound familiar? The governmental powers feared a loss of control and responded wickedly. So again, I ask, is this fiction or is this reality? My experience says that it certainly is a reality when it comes to the governing church bodies and the Dreamer of Dreams.

Yes, there are leaders in the church who do not and will not welcome the true "Dreamer of Dreams" out of fear of the meanings these dreams bring to their church bodies. So rather than accept the nature of the Dreamer's gift or "superpower" for what it is and allow it to be used for the purpose it serves, the very idea of the Dreamer of Dreams has been challenged and diminished. Like the superhero movies noted above, governing church leaders have tried to shut the dreamers up and make enemies out of them in an effort to discredit their power and motives so that they maintain the control they seek over the people. The church has pushed many dreamers into hiding, but the time has come for them to come out, as they are now being recalled by God while he deals with the church leaders among the body of Christ and their mismanagement of the Dreamer. God is trying to prepare the church for the Dreamer of Dreams, but because of the truth they will bring, the discomfort they will cause, and the power of interpretation they will walk in, the church will be threatened and will seemingly respond as the governmental powers did to the superheroes. The enemy has started a real attack on the Dreamer of Dreams because the time is coming when God will send dream upon dream to men and women to communicate His mind and heart to His people. Where there is truth, the enemy will attack, and the Dreamer of Dreams will dream God's truth in such a way that it can't be ignored.

It sounds outrageous to think that a leader would be so threatened by the truth out of fear of losing power that he/she would intentionally purpose to push the person exposing the truth into hiding so that what they are required to say is not heard or received. Sadly enough, and as extreme as it sounds, it's not exactly false. Nor is it a foreign concept.

There is a real villain in the Bible who specialized in just that—one who has survived all these years particularly in the church. Jezebel is her name. As I go deeper into this book, you will come to realize just how much of Jezebel is alive today as it concerns the Dreamer of Dreams and the depths that she will go to hold on to her power, using real-life stories that will blow you away. However, the main purpose in disclosing all that is shared in this book is to prepare the body and the world to receive the Dreamer, the dreams God sends, and to build the Dreamer up to tell the dream!

# CHAPTER TWO

# THE ORIGINS OF JEZEBEL

In Chapter 1, I mentioned the existence of real superheroes in the Bible. However, if there were indeed real superheroes living and operating in the Bible, then there also existed real villains. These villains, also mentioned earlier, could often be found in very high places of authority or "leadership positions" that gave them a great advantage to have and maintain great control over the land. Think about that for a minute. For example, in the book of Esther, Haman (who was honored and elevated by the king himself to a seat of honor higher than that of all the other nobles, as the Bible tells it) is identified as the main antagonist or villain to the Jews. Haman sought to have every living Jew destroyed, and because of his position with the king, he obtained the power to do so. In the book of Exodus, the Pharaoh who was ruler over Egypt became the chief villain who opposed the release of the Israelites from captivity. Saul, Amalek, King Agag, and the Pharisees were leaders, rulers, or kings who at one time or another were characterized as villains against the people of God. Yet, one of the most notorious Bible villains up to this very day was Jezebel; and this is due primarily to what she and her spirit represents, how often it attacks, and where you most frequently would encounter her.

## Jezebel: Who She Was

Jezebel was a Phoenician princess, daughter of Priest King Ethbaal, who was ruler of the coastal Phoenician cities Tyre and Sidon. Jezebel lived a pretty well-to-do life. After all, her father was the king of a thriving land. While the Phoenician people were a remarkable people, they engaged heavily in idol worship having no real regard for the "Great Jehovah." They worshipped many gods, the most important of which was Baal, the nature god. Consequently, Jezebel was raised in the same way, showing reverence and honor to Baal, Astarte, other gods, and to their priest or prophets, while giving no reverence or attention whatsoever to the "Great Jehovah." In an effort to create an alliance between Israel and Phoenicia, Jezebel was given in marriage to King Ahab to become queen.

## Jezebel: What She Did

King Ahab came from an entirely different culture than Jezebel. His land was not a thriving trading post full of businesses and wealth. His people didn't live the luxurious lifestyle Jezebel may have been accustomed to. But they were Great Jehovah worshippers. They believed in the concept of one God. Once the marriage between Ahab and Jezebel was official, Jezebel used her great influence to enforce her religious culture and beliefs on Ahab, thus infiltrating the whole country with idolatry and false prophets. Jezebel had such power and influence over Ahab that Ahab himself had 450 of her priests installed and placed in a temple that he had built for a "Sun-God" in Samaria. Another 400 were placed in a sanctuary that Jezebel also had built for them. As queen of Israel, Jezebel had the power and control she sought to implement her will over the people. And one of the main things she sought to do with this power was to convert Israel to Baal worship. Herein lies the evil plot of the story.

## Jezebel: Why Jezebel Does What She Does in the Land

The answer might shock you, but it is important to the message of this book. Jezebel does what she does because Jezebel doesn't think she's wrong. Let me say it to you like this. Do you recall the famous villain Darth Vader? Well if you follow the storyline of Star Wars, Darth Vader ultimately becomes Darth Vader because he believes it is the only way to save his wife and kids and restore balance in the galaxy. His intentions were to set order and stop an ongoing war. If that character is too far back for you to recall, let us analyze Thanos, the powerful villain pitted against the Avengers. Thanos pursues what becomes a murderous plot because he believes it is the only way to keep balance in the universe, allowing people to live better lives. In other words, the villain isn't the villain in the villain's eyes. The villain usually becomes the villain trying to prove why their methods are necessary. This is ultimately where you begin to see the fear tactics, intimidation tactics, manipulation tactics, power struggles, murderous plots, and so on imposed on innocent people.

Let's look at a real man, the Apostle Paul. At one time, Paul was going around persecuting and imprisoning anyone claiming to be a disciple of Jesus Christ. Paul wasn't doing this because he was evil, wicked-hearted, or fascinated with the idea of holding people captive against their will. He believed that the disciples' teachings were blasphemy. They went against everything he'd been taught, and he wanted to preserve his religious beliefs. So he went on a crusade to put away anyone who opposed his belief system.

Now let's look back to Jezebel. She believed wholeheartedly in her religious beliefs. Remember, Jezebel was raised to worship other gods, and as the daughter of a king, she was very committed and loyal to these beliefs. Would she just abandon these beliefs when they were all she knew to be right? She brought her paganism to Israel because she wanted them to partake in her belief system. From her perspective, it hadn't failed her yet. It hadn't cost her anything, and it was the cultural norm in her land. In fact, her land was prominently known for its great trading system, its luxurious purple dye, and the people's strong, thriving business skills. Israel was quite the opposite. Jezebel may have been inclined to believe that it was their religious beliefs that built and maintained her land to thrive as it did and that it was the very lack of that belief system that caused the land of Israel to look as it did to them. Like Paul, Jezebel wanted everyone to believe what she believed. After all, it could have been the turnaround Israel needed. Ultimately, what started from an innocent place ended up a murderous controlling spree because Jezebel wanted to preserve her religious beliefs and wanted others to believe as she did.

In Paul's case, when he was corrected through the power, voice, and demonstration of the Lord, he yielded. This was not the case with Jezebel as you will soon see. Paul was hungry for God, while Jezebel was hungry for power. Jezebel was stubborn. Jezebel did not like big change. She believed what she believed. She was true to tradition and her religious practices to the end, even when they opposed the will of God. Jezebel wanted what she wanted. She became so driven by her own desire that she turned into whomever and whatever she needed to be to see that desire fulfilled. She would do this even at the expense of other people's lives.

Now, this is something I wish for everyone to catch. You don't have to be wicked to become a Jezebel. Jezebel's initial actions did not come from a wicked place. They came from a traditional place and a place of religion. It was her inability to see the truth about the place she was in that caused her to become a great enemy of God—attacking, accusing, and intimidating the very servants sent by God to reveal the truth, expose God's truth, and break strongholds of spiritual bondage.

## Jezebel: Her Primary Enemy

As indicated above, where there is a villain, God will always raise up a superhero for the time of the attack. During this time, the real superheroes were the true Prophets of the true living God. The true Prophets of God became Jezebel's primary aim. She ordered that all of them were to be killed. It was from them that she felt her greatest threat. Why? They were never going to bow down to Baal worship. They were never going to be controlled as Ahab had been. They would continue to share the truth, the heart, and the mind of God, and through them God would demonstrate His power. They were going to always be a challenge because they could never just sit back and go with the flow of the land when it opposed the flow of God. The Prophets had the superpower to hear, interpret, and speak the mind and heart of God in a way that other men could not. They had a relationship with God that granted them access to successfully challenge Jezebel's actions in a way she could not ignore. Case in point, the Prophet Elijah.

While all the idolatry, immorality, and wicked intentions were flooding the land, Elijah appeared out of nowhere before the king and prophesied three years of drought. Drought hit the land. Then, sometime later, Elijah stepped back on the scene to challenge all 450 prophets of Baal that Jezebel had so forcefully worked to have brought into the land. He challenged them to a showdown in an effort to see whose God is really God. Elijah says:

> *Then Elijah said to them, "I am the only one of the LORD's prophets left, but Baal has four hundred and fifty prophets. Get two bulls for us. Let Baal's prophets choose one for themselves, and let them cut it into pieces and put it on the wood but not set fire to it. I will prepare the other bull and put it on the wood but not set fire to it. Then you call on the name of your god, and I will call on the name of the LORD. The god who answers by fire—he is God." Then all the people said, "What you say is good."*
> —1 Kings 18:22–24

The end result was catastrophic. The prophets of Baal began to call out to their pagan god through cries, dances, prayers, and shouts. They become so desperate for Baal to answer with the fire they were so badly seeking, that they began to slash themselves with swords and spears causing the blood to flow from their veins. Meanwhile, Elijah stood there observing and taunting them for their hopeless efforts: "At noon Elijah began to taunt them. 'Shout louder!' he said. 'Surely he is a god! Perhaps he is deep in thought, or busy, or traveling. Maybe he is sleeping and must be awakened'" (1 Kings 18:27).

After hours and hours of shouting, crying out, and cutting, the Baal prophets received no response. This went on morning and noon and all the way into the evening. Once Elijah had had enough, he gathered the people to him for a demonstration of his own through the power of God who is.

> *Then Elijah said to all the people, "Come here to me." They came to him, and he repaired the altar of the LORD, which had been torn down. Elijah took twelve stones, one for each of the tribes descended from Jacob, to whom the word of the LORD had come, saying, "Your name shall be Israel." With the stones he built an altar in the name of the LORD, and he dug a trench around it large enough to hold two seahs of seed. He arranged the wood, cut the bull into pieces and laid it on the wood. Then he said to them, "Fill four large jars with water and pour it on the offering and on the wood." "Do it again," he said, and they did it again. "Do it a third time," he ordered, and they did it the third time. The water ran down around the altar and even filled the trench.*

> *At the time of sacrifice, the prophet Elijah stepped forward and prayed: "LORD, the God of Abraham, Isaac and Israel, let it be known today that you are God in Israel and that I am your servant and have done all these things at your command. Answer me, LORD, answer me, so these people will know that you, LORD, are God, and that you are turning their hearts back again." Then the fire of the LORD fell and burned up the sacrifice, the wood, the stones and the soil, and also licked up the water in the trench.*

> —1 Kings 18:30–38

Through Elijah's God-given power, he was able to demonstrate whose God was really God. In other words, in front of an audience of many, he challenged the very order that Jezebel had attempted to set and proved it to be false, wrong, without truth, and self-willed. The audience responded only with worship to the one true living God despite Jezebel's wishes: "When all the people saw this, they fell prostrate and cried, 'The LORD—he is God! The LORD—he is God'" (1 Kings 18:39)!

If that wasn't bad enough in the eyes of Jezebel, Elijah then moved to have all 450 Baal prophets annihilated, and the people obeyed: "Then Elijah commanded them, 'Seize the prophets of Baal. Don't let anyone get away!' They seized them, and Elijah had them brought down to the Kishon Valley and slaughtered there" (1 Kings 18:40).

Imagine a superhero who emerges with enough power to completely change the order of things, even when it was commonly accepted by the people under the order or "under the heavy influence" to stay in the ungodly order. Elijah not only challenged Jezebel's order and the way she governed the people, but he also brought a powerful truth with him that could not be refuted because it was backed by powerful demonstrations done by the hand of God. People had no choice but to, at the very least, turn an eye to the God Elijah served despite the fear Jezebel had put in the land to serve her gods.

You see, Jezebel hated Elijah because he was a true prophet of the Lord whose mission was to expose the truth of God at all cost. It was not to blend in with the way things were run. He brought problems to Jezebel that put her in a position to be challenged by others.

Jezebel hated those who brought the truth, revelation, and the power of God that ultimately released people from strongholds of control, fear, intimidation, false beliefs, and manipulation. Ultimately, Jezebel wanted to keep people from seeing God and from seeing what they themselves were capable of should they be given the freedom to follow God in the way He had set for them. Modern-day Jezebel knows the people are free to do as they wish (even if they don't), but she aims to snatch away the freedom God has given them through the death of Jesus Christ so that they are never able to challenge the position of power she desires to maintain. Jezebel's enemy is anyone who challenges her with the truth of God and with the power of God.

## Jezebel: The Attack on Her Enemy

So how does Jezebel respond to those who oppose her? What is her plan of attack when the superheroes emerge out of their secret hiding place to challenge what she has been believed to be right all along? I'll tell you what she did according to the Bible. Jezebel put out an order to have all the true Prophets of the living God killed. All of them. And after the stunt Elijah pulled on her 450 prophets of Baal, she made Elijah a primary target, sending him into hiding and causing him to want to discontinue the good work God had set out for him.

> *Now Ahab told Jezebel everything Elijah had done and how he had killed all the prophets with the sword. So Jezebel sent a messenger to Elijah to say, "May the gods deal with me, be it ever so severely, if by this time tomorrow I do not make your life like that of one of them." Elijah was afraid and ran for his life. When he came to Beersheba in Judah, he left his servant there, while he himself went a day's journey into the wilderness. He came to a broom bush, sat down under it and prayed that he might die. "I have had enough, LORD," he said. "Take my life; I am no better than my ancestors." Then he lay down under the bush and fell asleep.*
>
> —1 Kings 19:1–5

Let's look at this for a moment. In this case, Jezebel's ideal strategy was to wipe her adversary out. Her aim was to cancel out the whole idea of him so that there would be no correction, no truth, no challenge, and no true demonstrations of God's power. Jezebel didn't want to befriend Elijah because he was too great a risk to her position of power. He couldn't be controlled. Jezebel didn't want to talk anything through with Elijah because she feared the truth. Therefore, Jezebel used intimidation and control to attack Elijah through her earthly power and position of authority, making him feel so uncomfortable about his gift that he didn't even desire to use it anymore. I will give a very true, real-life, modern-day example of this later in this book—one that is truly heart-stopping. But for now, let's look at another biblical scenario.

In another scenario, Jezebel also used other tactics such as retaliation, manipulation, and false accusation to attack her challengers to bring them to the point of death. Let's look at the story of Naboth. Naboth owned a vineyard that was in very close proximity to Ahab's palace. Ahab wanted the vineyard as his own to plant a vegetable garden, so he approached Naboth with a proposition. In short, Ahab proposed to purchase Naboth a better vineyard or give him money for the vineyard's worth in exchange for Naboth's current vineyard. Naboth, being well aware of his rights and the liberties allowed to him as a citizen in the land, declined King Ahab's offer. "But Naboth replied, 'The LORD forbid that I should give you the inheritance of my ancestors'" (1 Kings 21:3).

Unsurprisingly, Ahab, having no backbone of his own, goes away angry, sad, and upset and spills the beans to his tyrant wife, Jezebel. All Jezebel sees is that a man has challenged their authority. It doesn't matter that the man had the freedom and the right to exercise truth. It doesn't matter that what Naboth was saying was true. Jezebel's authority was challenged, and she could not allow that to get around to others. So Jezebel conjured up a plan to legally have Naboth put to death. Yes! She killed Naboth, but she killed him in a way that made her look justified in front of her people so that her actions could not be questioned.

*Jezebel his wife said, "Is this how you act as king over Israel? Get up and eat! Cheer up. I'll get you the vineyard of Naboth the Jezreelite." So she wrote letters in Ahab's name, placed his seal on them, and sent them to the elders and nobles who lived in Naboth's city with him. In those letters she wrote:*

*"Proclaim a day of fasting and seat Naboth in a prominent place among the people. But seat two scoundrels opposite him and have them bring charges that he has cursed both God and the king. Then take him out and stone him to death." So the elders and nobles who lived in Naboth's city did as Jezebel directed in the letters she had written to them. They proclaimed a fast and seated Naboth in a prominent place among the people. Then two scoundrels came and sat opposite him and brought charges against Naboth before the people, saying, "Naboth has cursed both God and the king." So they took him outside the city and stoned him to death. Then they sent word to Jezebel: "Naboth has been stoned to death."*

—1 Kings 21:7–14

Let's dissect this for a moment. Jezebel called a fast. She used a religious practice to deploy a manipulative plan of action. She then enticed Naboth by seating him in a position of importance in front of the people. In other words, Jezebel hid behind religion to keep her hands looking clean while she was manipulating the situation to work for her own selfish motives. She flattered Naboth. She gave him just enough power, attention, and recognition to keep him under control, and she did all this to draw an audience that would be in favor of her. Jezebel knew how to put on a show. Then, once her audience was captivated, she had men make false accusations on her target publicly so that she would be justified to bring Naboth down. Essentially, all of what Jezebel did was to silence the truth and keep people locked in spiritual bondage.

This is why she responded with the intensity that she did against Elijah and Naboth. Elijah had a powerful gift that got the attention of the people, and it threatened Jezebel's order and way of running things. Jezebel resented being made to believe anything was wrong with the way she ran her system because her system had worked great for her. Naboth was a demonstration of the danger a man walking in liberty could be to Jezebel's system. Therefore, anyone walking in their power and their freedom to exercise that power became Jezebel's primary target.

Up to now, we have spoken of Jezebel in the past tense, but rest assured Jezebel isn't done yet. Her spirit is lurking within the governing bodies of the body of Christ and she's prepared to discredit, make false accusation, set aside, silence, and destroy whoever poses a challenge to her. However, the time has come for her to face one of her greatest superhero adversaries of all times for the end-times: the Dreamer of Dreams. I like to refer to them, now, and herein, as the "Dreamsmen," and it will be a real showdown because of the power, the revelation, and the truth of the dream.

# CHAPTER THREE

# DREAMSMEN: JEZEBEL'S NEW ENEMY

My heart was pounding in my chest. The blood was racing through my veins. There had to be hundreds of butterflies floating all through my stomach. Here I was at work, pacing my classroom in disbelief at what I was actually working up my nerves to do.

Dionne entered the classroom with her co-teacher and class, and I knew then that it had to be done. I waited for the right moment; then I said, "Excuse me, Miss Dionne. This is about to be really crazy—what I am about to say—since we have no kind of relationship outside of you dropping your class off to my room for music every week, but I had a really detailed dream about you the other night that I really feel is incumbent on me to share with you. Is there a time, maybe during your break, that we can talk over this dream? I really believe you are supposed to hear this dream now." Dionne looked over to her co-teacher with a look of amazement. Her co-teacher responded to her facial expression by saying, "O-M-G, you just said you needed a sign. Maybe this is it."

Dionne looked back over to me with great anticipation and said, "I can come to you during my lunch break. I really want to hear this." So, we agreed on the time and the meeting place, and I knew that I had reached the point of no return. Both the dream and the interpretation were going to be shared; there was no turning back.

It was 1:00 p.m. The time had come. Here I was not even knowing if she would even receive me. I didn't even know what she believed. But I had this dream that was way too vivid and descriptive to ignore burning on my heart. I knew something that I had to make known to Dionne.

Because I had an empty room, Dionne would meet me right where I was. At about 1:05 p.m., Dionne knocked on the door. I let her in and pulled her up a chair near me. In an attempt to calm my nerves, I began to share with Dionne the gift I was given for dreams. I explained to her that it is one very primary way that God communicates things that He needs communicated through me and to me, and though it scares me to death at times to go out on a limb and share these dreams with people I am not very familiar with, I have to do so. I went on to tell her that the dream I was about to tell her was going to sound very weird and ridiculous and that she would need to wait for the interpretation to truly understand it. All the while I was reading her body language, facial expressions, and anything else that would tell me whether this was going to go over well. Surprisingly, for someone who I had never said more than hello and goodbye to, she was very welcoming and warm. This lightened me up a whole lot. It was time to dive in, and so I did:

> The dream started out with you in a bathtub. Ashton Kutcher was sitting on the side of the tub as you were preparing to present yourself to him. But it was clear you lacked the confidence, and as a result, you allowed yourself to be taken advantage of hoping that at some point your talent or your gift would be recognized. Ashton detected your lack of confidence and used it to his advantage, but you never were given the opportunity

you were seeking, and it made you feel lower. Then the dream transitioned, and you and I were at this high-end charity event with rich millionaires. You were dressed in this amazing sparkling dress that was evidently given to you by this elderly Caucasian couple whom you escorted to the function. Somehow, my observations led me to believe you were sleeping with this elderly Caucasian man and that his wife knew. You didn't like it, but they kept money in your pocket, and you felt it was what would land you where you wanted to be. All the while I could see you dying in this place. You were not becoming you, but this elderly Caucasian couple had you on a leash, and they were continuously thriving because of what you could do for them.

I eventually pulled you to the side and I whispered in your ear, "I know what they are doing to you. You are so much better than this, and there is so much more God wants to do with you, but you have got to break away from their grip." You began to cry, and you admitted everything to me expressing your desire to break away. You then agreed to follow me discreetly to a safe place away from the party. In this safe place, you started singing, and you sang so freely and so well. It was as if you were an entirely different person. This is where the dream ended.

Of course, she looked at me with great intensity for what this all meant, and I knew by the look on her face and by the attentiveness to my words that something in that dream resonated in her heart. She was undoubtedly ready for the interpretation. I explained to her in a calm but confident tone that she lacked a great confidence in the gifts and talents that God had given her and because of that, she had allowed herself to sit too long overlooked in places God had called her away from. At this point I knew I had crossed over into a different place with her, and I had to finish what I had started even if it made absolutely no sense.

I went on boldly to tell her how she had allowed herself to be continuously taken advantage of over and over again. "You are not literally a sex slave to this couple, but you and your gifts have become a slave to the couple who owns this school" (the place where she was currently employed). Tears began to well up in her eyes. She could no longer keep them from falling. As the tears rolled down her cheek, I proceeded to tell her the interpretation:

> I am here to tell you to freely move forward in the gifts that God has given you to your safe place. That's what gives you life, but you can't do it tied up here. You see this as your livelihood when in actuality, it is stunting your destiny. You were sitting in the bathtub hoping what you had done so far and what you had allowed to be done to you would lead you to be accepted, valued, and sincerely recognized where you wanted to be, but it only kept you from being. Make the decision to move.

Dionne was not the only one who was literally baffled that day. What she said next, not only shocked me, but it provided even more clarity to the dream. With tears in her eyes and from a place of bewilderment, Dionne said to me:

> You don't know this about me, which is crazy, but I have been pursuing acting and singing for some time. (This was what Ashton Kutcher represented, acting.) Now, I just feel like I'm in a stuck place because being here at this school gives me absolutely no time or freedom to do what I know I need to do. I knew a long time ago I was supposed to leave here. I even tried to cut back on

my hours and become a sub, but every time I made the decision to do less here or leave, the owners enticed me with something better to keep me here. They made me feel bad for leaving. So to keep them happy or to keep from disappointing them, I stayed. In the meantime, I am not moving forward with any of who I am. I was just telling my coworker that it is time for me to go.

She said this as if she was really understanding something for the first time. Then, after making countless efforts to stop crying and having to fight through tears, she said:

I don't know why I can't stop crying. I am so sorry. I don't cry like this. I didn't mean to cry like this. I just can't believe you are saying this to me right now when this is exactly what I was asking God about. Thank you so much. I know what I have to do.

Can you conceptualize the idea that a dream, a simple dream, could be the very resolution that shuts down the plot of the enemy? Or that it could be the very insight that causes people to avoid faulty or destructive decisions? Or that it can bring the revelation that can change the whole operation of things? Or that it can be the very key that frees a person from any form of captivity so that they can fully pursue their purpose? Or that it can reveal the hidden truths behind people's motives and actions? It may be difficult for the average person to conceptualize, but it isn't difficult for Dreamsmen or for a Jezebel who has been challenged by one.

Dreams have been minimized as being nothing short of a natural occurrence that takes place every now and then in the average human being. In many cases, they are seen as expressions of the subconscious mind. In other words, because you are going through something, your mind, through dream form, can express your inner thoughts and feelings about the situation. Likewise, if you watch a movie and go to sleep with that movie on your mind, you are likely to dream something relatively close to it. This may be true for many, but there are some individuals who have been given a distinct ability to dream outside of the norm. They do not dream from their own mind or from their own heart—but from the heart and mind of God to position God's people into their kingdom purposes. I call these beings "Dreamsmen."

They have been built up to see whatever God needs them to see even if in waking life they see differently. Case in point: in the dream about Dionne. Dionne dropped her class off to my classroom every Thursday morning. Under no circumstances was there any communication between us that indicated that she was in a pivotal place in her life in which she was waiting for a sign to determine whether she would make her exit to really flourish in the things she was most passionate about. Yet, as a Dreamsmen, the real picture was illustrated for me to, not only give insight on the true value of her gifts, but to provide her an outlook of God's perspective of the damage being done to her emotionally, physically, and spiritually every time she made the conscious decision to stay.

Dreamsmen do not need to talk to anybody or think up anything. Nor is their gift to dream affected by their own situations. They are just custom-made to see. Not only are they custom-made to see, but they are custom-made to interpret what they see.

It's like this. Everybody can sing as long as they have a voice to do so. It does not, however, mean that everyone has the gift to sing well or that everyone has the ability to interpret perfect pitch when singing. Furthermore, a person's gift to sing isn't affected by the kind of day they're having or their subconscious mind or what they watched before they sang if they truly know how to sing. In addition, a person who becomes an expert at using their gift to sing would know how to treat the gift, nurture the gift, and develop the gift for its best use, minimizing opportunities for malfunction, and they would easily be able to recognize a good note from a bad one or when a note just doesn't fit.

Now let's look at this from the Dreamsmen's perspective. I do believe that everyone will experience some form of a dream. It does not mean, however, that everyone has a gift to dream or interpret as Dreamsmen do. Likewise, Dreamsmen's dreams very rarely have anything to do with their kind of day, their subconscious mind, themselves, or the target of their focus before they go to sleep. Why? Because nine times out of 10, they dream the heart and mind of God as opposed to their very own. And finally, because expert Dreamsmen have been dreaming for quite some time, they understand how to take care of the gift, nurture the gift, and develop the gift for its best use, minimizing opportunities for malfunctions. And of course, they are easily able to recognize a God-dream from a man-dream from a dark-dream. They understand the nature of their gift and seek to use it with caution. For Dreamsmen, what becomes difficult is the dream itself. Why? Because oftentimes, the dream has no strong point of reference in the waking world. Dreamsmen dream in a way that has nothing to do with the world around them. They dream according to what God wants them to know concerning the world around them from a spiritual perspective. To put it simpler, dreams give the real version of the story being told or being lived in the waking world.

Biblically speaking, dreams give divine insight and direction concerning the plans of God even when they are in complete contrast with what is presently taking place in the waking world. They provide divine instruction that aligns people with the will of God—instruction that others might consider to be the most irrational thing to do. They prepare people for what's to come even when the waking world shows no sign of the occurrence revealed in the dream. They provide warnings and correction where there seems to be no need for either in the waking world. They are used to avoid costly situations that in the waking world may not seem costly at all. They direct your attention to where God needs your attention to be, especially when you're missing exactly where the attention should be. Finally, they give God's perspective on a situation or the truth about a situation. In other words, they give the real behind-the-scenes look at how God sees everything, even when what is visible in the waking world doesn't appear to need a closer look.

So you see, dreams are powerful offensive mechanisms designed to lead people in the purpose of the Lord while keeping them alert against the things that would derail them from His purpose. Dreams break bondages and serve as God's light even in the dark. Although Dionne had logically concluded that her job was necessary, the dream revealed that her job was the primary derailing factor that kept her from achieving purpose. Knowing this freed her to go forward and become. That is powerful.

So why are dreams undervalued? Why don't we take the time to understand dreams? Why don't we seek experts to diagnose dreams?

Dreams are still one of God's most powerful methods of communication. And with dreams, you don't have to be uncertain about what you heard because you saw it. Therein lies the threat to Jezebel.

Everything God does with a dream, Jezebel does the opposite. Jezebel wants control. The dream frees. Jezebel wants all the power. The dream gives power. Jezebel hides behind a show. The dream sees the truth behind the show. Jezebel leads you into bondage or captivity, stagnating you from purpose. The dream walks you directly into the line of purpose. Jezebel makes false accusations to kill the gift. The dream uses truth to edify and validate the gift. Jezebel is religious. The dream is God. Jezebel seeks to tie you down with traditional practices and religious works. The dream aligns you to God's line of work. Now, read this paragraph over again, but put it in the context of the Dionne dream. This dream was everything Jezebel hated, and this dream was used to undo for Dionne everything Jezebel had done to Dionne.

Dreamsmen are the primary adversary for Jezebel because like Elijah's demonstration of power before the 450 prophets of Baal, the dream itself strongly reveals and is often too difficult to refute. How did they know this? How did they see this? Why are they seeing this? What else will they be shown? Why won't they just do what I am asking?

Jezebel fears the Dreamsmen because of the power of the dream. Jezebel acts out in the face of the Dreamsmen because of their power to see the dream. That is, the dream will keep people from under the control of man and place them under the hand and protection of God. Later in this book, you will read some real-life demonstrations of Jezebel's attack against Dreamsmen. For right now, however, let's use the next chapter to demonstrate and reflect on the power of the dream.

# CHAPTER FOUR

# THE DREAM-DREAMSMEN'S FIRST SUPERPOWER

In the previous chapter, I stated:

> Biblically speaking, dreams give divine insight and direction concerning the plans of God even when they are in complete contrast with what is in the waking world. They provide divine instruction that aligns people with the will of God—instruction that others might consider to be the most irrational thing to do. They prepare people for what's to come even when the waking world shows no sign of the occurrence revealed in the dream. They provide warnings and correction where there seems to be no need for either in the waking world. They are used to avoid costly situations that in the waking world may not seem costly at all. They direct your attention to where God needs your attention to be, especially when you're missing exactly where the attention should be. They give God's perspective on a situation, or the truth about a situation. Or in other words, they give the real behind-

the-scenes look at how God sees everything, even when what is visible in the waking world doesn't appear to need a closer look.

Now let's dissect each dream objective for truth, one objective at a time.

1. *Dreams give divine insight and direction concerning the plans of God even when they are in complete contrast with what is presently taking place in the waking world.* In the Bible, it was through the form of a dream that Abraham was reminded that his wife would give birth to a son and that he would be the father of many nations. I might add that his wife was barren and about 90 years of age when this dream came about. As ridiculous as it seemed in the natural, God made His plan clear to Abraham by way of a dream. This dream gave divine insight about a divinely orchestrated plan that in no way aligned with the way things were in waking life, but it was the plan that came into existence shortly after. How about that! A God-given dream doesn't retrieve its knowledge from present worldly conditions.

Similarly, I had a dream in which God showed me a ministerial colleague of mine standing before a prominent government council that had international influence. (My friend was a national trainer in sales and marketing and had been in that field most of her professional career.) These government officials seemed to have the authority to develop and create programs and make legislative decisions concerning what was necessary for change all over the globe. Having heard about some of my ministerial colleague's work in an unfamiliar area of youth and civic work, they sent for her and stood her in front of them to offer her a position within their council, though they were well aware that she had no governmental or matching degree experience.

I woke up the morning after this dream, and I could not wait to call her. While I knew that what I saw in the dream completely went against where she was professionally as a national sales and marketing trainer in corporate America, I also knew without a doubt what I saw was real. I called my friend and excitingly said, "It's the mountain of government that God is going to blossom you!" Without even listening for a response, I went on to share with her in the most electrifying tone the full dream, emphasizing that her experience didn't matter and that she was just being positioned to be exactly what the government needed. Keep in mind while I am giving her this exhilarating news, she has absolutely no governmental experience, no governmental access, no governmental degrees, no governmental time, no governmental contacts, no governmental anything to tie her to this crazy illogical dream I was bringing to her. Be that as it may, she gently responded to me and said, "I don't see it, but I receive it."

Months later, an official from the mayor's council of Atlanta, Georgia, took note of my colleague's work with youth through her nonprofit work, and despite her lack of experience or associated degrees, she was given the title of program chair for the Ready for Success Initiative under the governmental department of constituent services. Since this dream, she has landed contracts with the Department of Juvenile Justice and sat in as chair for countless governmental meetings, leading citywide initiatives for youth. When she received her first governmental contract, she called me to say, "You said it would be government. At the time I didn't see it, but I do now."

2. *They provide divine instruction that aligns people with the will of God—instruction that others may consider to be the most irrational thing to do.* A great biblical example would be when God shared with Joseph, by way of dream, not to divorce Mary because she was carrying the Savior of the world. Here it is again—dreams clash with logic and go completely against the way of the world. Joseph's wife was pregnant, and evidently, she had conceived long before her marriage to Joseph. In fact, Joseph hadn't even had the opportunity to consummate the marriage before he realized that his wife was pregnant. Therefore, unlike some of the men on *The Maury Show*, Joseph knew this baby did not belong to him. To Joseph and anyone else, Mary had committed a grave sin. According to tradition, Mary should have been put to death. Essentially,

that would be the most logical and legitimate instruction of all. But then comes the "dream" that goes totally against that instruction and gives the most nonreligious, nontraditional, irrational instruction of all: "Stay married to Mary. She is carrying the Savior of the world."

Would you believe me if I told you that God used a dream to show me my second husband while I was still married to my first? Although my first husband truly struggled with monogamy and put the family and me in some dangerous situations because of his infidelities, this dream brought me to shame. Why would I dream this? And why him? Despite what the marriage was doing to me, I did not want to let it go. I had four children with my first husband, and I wanted the marriage to work. "Why, God, would you allow me to see this?" My mind was far from anything like this. I was so embarrassed by this, I wouldn't share the dream with anyone at the time. But this is what I have come to know. God-given dreams aren't subject to the control, thoughts, or systems of man, and they make their audiences uncomfortable at times because they go against tradition and religious mindsets. Oftentimes, dreams go against the majority. I understand what Mary's Joseph was going through, being given a dream that no one would understand or perceive as being from God. Who would believe that God said to stay married to someone the world perceived to be an "adulterous woman"?

This was hard for me because nothing about this dream seemed normal. Nothing about it, according to man, seemed right. Here I am dreaming a dream that has me holding hands with my husband's relative and walking in a Walmart parking lot. Then he looks at me and says, "Are you ready to do this?" I look back at him and say, "Yes." Then he says, "You know we're going to take a lot of hits from the people for this, but I'm with you, and we are going to make it through together." The crazier thing is how I felt during the dream. There was such a peace—a knowledge that all was well and that all would be well as long as we walked together. It was a feeling I couldn't shake. But it was a feeling I would do everything in my power to shake and a dream I would bury without anyone's knowledge.

I wasn't mature enough then to fully understand what was going on. But I now understand that what God had allowed me to experience was similar to Samuel being told to anoint David as the new king while Saul was still the king. I didn't want to accept that my first husband was fired, and although God had already made the decision, I struggled, like Samuel, to accept it. While I was wrestling with the idea, God was already anointing my David, and He gave me a glimpse into the process. Everyone didn't know what Samuel truly came down to Jesse's to do, just as everyone didn't know truly what God was bringing Mike, my husband today, down to do, but God always reveals his plans to someone. In this case, He revealed it to me, a Dreamsmen.

I went through a very strenuous divorce that both broke me and built me. But I would come to know this particular Walmart dream as my Joseph dream, so that two and a half years later, when God said to me, "Marry him; Marry Mike," I would remember that this was already ordained, and I wouldn't let all the accusations and the opinions of men offset me from what was purposed by God. Almost three years after the dream, that man walking in the parking lot with me became my husband. And, God has blessed us with two more children, a powerful flourishing ministry, prosperous works of our hands, and a spiritual walk that has blown our minds year after year.

You see, it was that dream that helped me to stay on the irrational side where God was when others tried to sit me on the rational side where man was. And if you're wondering the significance of us being in a Walmart parking lot, let me help you a bit. After being divorced almost three years and subconsciously trying to keep a dream buried, it was in the Walmart parking lot in Fayetteville, Georgia, where I heard the voice of God so clearly say, "And now, I release you to marry him." My husband and I didn't date. We didn't investigate or try to make heads or tails of it. Somehow, we both just knew, and we were married exactly a month after the "Walmart" experience.

3. *They prepare people for what's to come even when the waking world shows no sign of the occurrence revealed in the dream.* One morning, I woke up from a horrifying dream. A fire had suddenly broken out next to a huge truck and while people had their attention on the fire, I was taking notice that the ground was suddenly cracking underneath us. I saw that in a matter of moments, the whole ground would cave in under us. I tried to warn the people to get to the other side of the road where it was safe before the fall. Fortunately, we were able to move fast enough, and everyone was able to make it to the other side just before the ground completely collapsed. When I awoke from this dream, the Spirit of the Lord spoke to me and urged me to share this dream on social media. I understood that what I had seen in my dream the previous night, the world would see in a very short time. My role was to make the announcement so that people would believe.

I struggled with that because I knew that a "short time" to us, does not equate to a "short time" to God. I didn't want to make that kind of announcement only to have people looking at me like I was crazy because nothing like this was taking place anytime soon. Eventually, my own logical mind had its way, and I settled in my heart and in my mind that I would not reveal or announce this dream on any social media outlet. This dream stayed between me and my husband.

You'll never believe what took place later on that day! Yes. A fire broke out on I-85 in Atlanta, Georgia, and while the proper authorities were being called to put the fire out, that part of I-85 collapsed. And it happened minutes before anyone was hurt. Lesson learned.

This dream told exactly what was about to happen and even provided insight on how the fire would serve as a distraction to what was the real danger at a time when no one would expect it. Likewise, God provided this same type of insight through Joseph's interpretation of Pharaoh's dream concerning the seven years of abundance and the seven years of famine. Because God had given Pharaoh a dream showing that immediately after seven years of abundance, the land would experience seven years of extreme famine, Joseph understood what to do during the seven years of abundance. Joseph understood that the seven years of abundance were not a time to squander resources and live lavishly but to conserve, put away, and store up what they would need through the upcoming famine. In both cases God warned the dreamer to prepare for the occurrence that would happen after the initial occurrence so that one occurrence wouldn't lead to a fatal outcome in the other.

4. *They provide warnings and correction where there seems to be no need for either in the waking world.* One time, there was a member in my congregation who was one of the most helpful people I knew. Anything she could help me with she did whether it was business, my children, or the ministry. She operated to a certain degree as an armor-bearer and a servant, so she had great access into all the areas of my life and the life of my husband. In fact, she was a tad bit closer to my husband because it was my husband who introduced her and a few more of his coworkers to our ministry. This young lady would say to me on several occasions, "You guys saved my life." She was like a godsend, and my family welcomed her with open arms. We even went so far as to refer to her as a "Senior." She and my husband, who were both of Jamaican descent, would refer to each other as sister and brother. If she had a need, my husband and I would make it a point to do our part to try to meet it. All seemed well.

Then came the dream. In this dream my husband and I were in our bedroom doing the ministry that husbands and wives do in the bedroom. While we are engaging in the act, in walks our "Senior" friend with our baby. I think to myself, surely, she's going to walk out having realized what she walked in on, but she would not leave the room. She didn't feel compelled to leave, and she felt justified in staying. She literally stood by the bed and watched. I knew at the end of the dream that we had given her way too much access into our home and that we would need to make some boundaries clear, but it didn't end there.

Within two or three days of that dream, I dreamed that it had been exposed that our "Senior" friend had intimate feelings for my husband that she had planned on revealing to him. Somehow, I found out first and was able to tell my husband, in the dream of course, that our "Senior" friend wanted to be with him. My husband surprisingly became torn about how to gently turn her away without ruining their close friendship. I couldn't understand his need to be gentle when she was making a choice to disrespect our family by pursuing a relationship with him, and this caused very bad tension between us.

I woke up and I shared this dream with my husband. Between the two dreams, it became very clear to me that the closeness we thought we had with our friend stemmed from other motives. And we, apparently, had given her the access she needed to do what was really inside of her to do all along. Unlike the dream, however, my husband wanted to do whatever he needed to ensure that she would never, ever feel comfortable enough to tell him something like that. So, in waking life, my husband began to pursue actions to guard himself and our family from such an occurrence. What did that look like? Well, he stopped her from just dropping in whenever she wanted whether I was home or not. He would no longer use her to babysit our youngest kids, and he significantly reduced the amount of phone time he would give to her. Simply put, anything that wasn't me and her, he significantly reduced, and in some cases blatantly stopped. This seemed a little harsh to me. After all, she didn't know what I had dreamed, and maybe her feelings weren't there yet. But I soon came to realize how real that dream was.

You see, the less time my husband spent with her, the nastier she became with me. Her entire work ethic changed. Her kindness turned into coldness and rudeness. Her willingness to help turned into sabotage as she made attempts to draw others away from me, the business, and the ministry. One could say as soon as she saw her plan to take my husband was no longer moving in the direction she hoped, her true self was exposed. Ultimately, she left the ministry and any of the work tied to it, and she never spoke to either one of us again.

In this case, the dreams served as warnings correcting us and our actions against something our hearts would not have allowed us to see coming. We liked the way everything was flowing because it all seemed to be flowing well, but the way it was flowing was not to our benefit. Had it not been for the power of the dream, I truly believe my marriage would have faced a level of opposition that we may not have been ready for so early in the ministry.

This reminds me of Abimelech's warning in the Bible. Here Abraham was passing off his wife, Sarah, as his sister, and Abimelech was thinking she was available, but the dream said don't touch her. Of course, to Abimelech at first glance, there was absolutely no harm in pursuing Sarah, but a dream corrected his thoughts and plans of action so that devastating events did not follow.

5. *They are used to avoid costly situations that in the waking world may not seem costly at all.* I once heard a prophetic teacher say, "A dream is just a dream until it manifests." I wanted to agree out of great respect and admiration, but I couldn't because all dreams are not meant to manifest. Some dreams are meant to warn us against what could manifest should we remain oblivious to the dream just as my previous dream did. There are dreams that God allows us to see and experience to help us avoid the very costly manifestation of them, and it is up to us to take good notes during the dream experience so that we know what actions to take when we wake.

Case in point: In Daniel chapter 4, Nebuchadnezzar has a dream that Daniel interpreted in this way:

> *This is the interpretation, Your Majesty, and this is the decree the Most High has issued against my lord the king: You will be driven away from people and will live with the wild animals; you will eat grass like the ox and be drenched with the dew of heaven. Seven times will pass by for you until you acknowledge that the Most High is sovereign over all kingdoms on earth and gives them*

*to anyone he wishes. The command to leave the stump of the tree with its roots means that your kingdom will be restored to you when you acknowledge that Heaven rules.*

—Dan. 4:24–26

Daniel gives a full description of a horrible occurrence that is to be manifested as a lesson to Nebuchadnezzar for his lack of reverence and acknowledgment of the hand of God in his life. Because he chooses to take all the credit for what God has done, God is about to allow him, for lack of better words, to go insane. Now at this point, God has only allowed Nebuchadnezzar, by way of Daniel's interpretation, to see what will be, but he also provides instruction through Daniel in an attempt to help him avoid the full manifestation of what he has seen and heard concerning the dream. Daniel ends his interpretation by suggesting to Nebuchadnezzar that he should renounce his sins. Daniel pretty much says, in so many words, "That could be what saves you from this major moment of insanity."

*Therefore, Your Majesty, be pleased to accept my advice: Renounce your sins by doing what is right, and your wickedness by being kind to the oppressed. It may be that then your prosperity will continue.*

—Dan. 4:27

The Bible tells us that nothing happened to Nebuchadnezzar for 12 months. But then he does exactly what he was advised against. He says, "Is not this the great Babylon I have built as the royal residence, by my mighty power and for the glory of my majesty" (Daniel 4:30)? Then it happens. The full manifestation of the dream comes to fruition. Nebuchadnezzar is stripped of his royal authority and driven away from people to eat grass like an ox.

*Even as the words were on his lips, a voice came from heaven, "This is what is decreed for you, King Nebuchadnezzar: Your royal authority has been taken from you. You will be driven away from people and will live with the wild animals; you will eat grass like the ox. Seven times will pass by for you until you acknowledge that the Most High is sovereign over all kingdoms on earth and gives them to anyone he wishes." Immediately what had been said about Nebuchadnezzar was fulfilled. He was driven away from people and ate grass like the ox. His body was drenched with the dew of heaven until his hair grew like the feathers of an eagle and his nails like the claws of a bird.*

—Dan. 4:31–33

Did this dream have to manifest? No, it didn't. Did Nebuchadnezzar take good notes and respond accordingly? No, he didn't, but the dream certainly had given him the opportunity. God would rather show us his mercy than his wrath on any given day, and sometimes, that is just what dreams are—opportunities to come correct in an effort to spare us from what could be. That is only possible if we respect them enough to take notice.

I wanted so bad to justifiably go completely off on a woman who I felt deserved all of what I had in me to give. I wanted to forget all righteous words. I wanted to put down all godly principles, and I wanted to just let loose one good time. But I knew that it was all a trap. My testimony, my character—all that God was building in me—would be killed, destroyed, eradicated, and questioned. Ask me how I knew? I dreamed it, and I took notes.

Two days before my whole life was tried by one individual, I dreamed I was sitting in a classroom only to have some classmates who knew who I was spiritually make false accusations of me. Their goal was to challenge everything God had said I was, and they wanted to prove it all false by making a public demonstration. They provoked, laughed, taunted, kept up trouble so that I would not focus on the teacher but on them. I tried so hard to stay focused on the teacher. I mean, I couldn't even understand why the teacher was allowing this in the first place. He saw what they were doing, but he never silenced them. I was just sitting there hearing it, taking it, and coming to a place where I would no longer fight it.

All of sudden, I stood up, knocked over the desk, and cursed out the ringleader and all her stooges. I had no control. I lost it. I went all the way off, only to have the ringleader look at me and say, "See, ya'll, I told you; she was just like us." I could feel my heart sink into my chest. What had I just done? I had killed my whole testimony. My character was on display, and I had failed. The classmates taunting me immediately left the room satisfied that they had accomplished their mission. The teacher walked up to me and sat at a desk next to me and said to me, "That isn't who you are. I know who you are. Don't you allow them to take you to that place ever again."

I woke up. I knew that I was about to be tried in such a way that it would have my blood boiling, but I had been prepared, and it was my responsibility to represent Christ no matter what because the enemy was after my character. Two days later, it happened. An in-law unexpectedly flew in from out of the country and started all kinds of chaos within the family, making me her primary target. She attacked me as a mother, a wife, a woman, and a woman of God. As I took those false accusations built on a foundation of lies, all I could think of was what had happened in the dream and what the teacher had said. I had been prepared not to fail. And I didn't. Not one wicked word, action, or tone emerged out of me. I gave the enemy absolutely nothing to work with because God had prepared me through the dream. I showed love, I showed godly character, and I walked away in peace.

6. *They direct your attention to where God needs your attention to be, especially when you're missing exactly where the attention should be.* As a Pastor, I involve all my children in the ministry. One of my

daughters is a praise and worship leader. For the most part, she had come to a point in her young life in which she was worshipping God freely. She was watching her tone with her siblings. She had corrected an issue she had with talking back. She was tremendously helpful around the house. She seemed to successfully come out of what could have been a destructible pathway, and the family could not have been prouder. So we stopped watching her with the same intensity as we once did. As far as me, my husband, her grandparents, and our circle of association were concerned, my daughter had finally gotten it. And then, the dream.

This dream was so frightening. This dream was so real. This dream was full of emotions I could feel deep down in my soul. My daughter had died. And before she took her last breath, she told me over a phone, "Mommy, it's okay. I know why I am dying." She went on to tell me how she had been playing two sides for too long and that she knew God had to put a stop to it His way. Then she was gone. She was no longer on the phone, and I knew she was no longer walking the earth. I screamed in agony. I began to blame myself for not getting to the heart of what was really going on with her. I kept telling my husband who was trying so hard to console me, "I should have been sterner about it. I should have done it differently. I will never hear her voice again." My husband kept trying to tell me this was how God chose to do it. But I couldn't accept this. It was just too devastating.

When I woke up from this dream, I knew God wanted my undivided attention on my daughter. He wanted to bring to light everything she was "still" involved in even though it appeared like everything was well. Without any hesitation I immediately called out to my daughter, and I shared the dream with her. I explained to her that this was not the time to pretend. "Whatever you are involved in," I said, "you need to confess it, so we can deal with it, because if it doesn't stop, your life will be abruptly taken." My daughter was frightened. She began to break down and cry, and then she confessed things no one in the family would have ever imagined she had been involved in. This dream saved my daughter's life. While our attention was on other areas, God brought it back to what was urgent to Him. Only the dream turned our attention around to what was necessary at that moment.

7. *They give God's perspective on a situation, or the truth about a situation. Or in other words, they give the real behind-the-scenes look at how God sees everything, even when what is visible in the waking world doesn't appear to need a closer look.* I know an older woman who I will refer to as Mrs. Jones. She has served in her ministry faithfully for over 15 years. By that I mean she not only attended the regular weekly Sunday services but also everything in between. Wherever there was a need, she faithfully served where she could. Of course, being a member for so long, she had seen plenty—a lot of good and a lot of bad. Some of the bad has been devastating for others and, in some cases, for her. She used to be a challenging voice in the body, but it kept her in an uncomfortable place and, at times, at odds with her leadership. So, she learned how to stay quiet, neutral, and submissive in an effort to keep peace with those around her. She learned how to keep her leaders content. She even encouraged others to do the same.

While she achieved the peace, comfort, and neutrality she sought in the ministry, she did not fully operate at the level for which she had been called. Nevertheless, she prayed, she worshipped, she served, and she learned to adjust and be whatever was necessary for the vision of her Pastors to go forth. Her Pastors loved her. Her ministry accepted her. That's what it was all about, right? Surely, God was pleased. Or not.

I dreamed about Mrs. Jones, having had no real contact with her for over five years. Yet, this dream painted a totally different picture of Mrs. Jones and what she represented. The scary part of it all was that this dream came from the perspective of God.

The dream took place in a huge facility. There was nothing inside the facility but the poles that served as the foundation to hold it up and thousands of people. There were three kinds of people in the facility. The first group of people were masked soldiers. They walked throughout the facility carrying guns. Their mission was to keep people from escaping the facility. They used their guns to intimidate and oppress the people so that the people would not even think of trying to get out of this "gigantic cage." There was a second group of people who were not soldiers. However, they would literally stay in one place, hold their head down, and walk around in tiny circles. They were positioned all over the facility doing this. I had quickly come to realize that they were doing what the masked soldiers was requiring them to do. To add to the soldiers' objective, they were to make sure the people walked around in circles with their heads down so that they never saw their way out, and they were never able to move out from where they were. Finally, there was a third group of people. They were not soldiers. They were not walking around in circles. They were gathering together in preparation to fight their way out.

I appeared to be the corporal leading and planning the attack. We found a hidden place to meet, and we strategized. Then, it was time for the attack. We knew we were outnumbered; we didn't have guns, but we knew we could not stay there. So we fought. We were not just fighting for our freedom but ultimately for the freedom of everyone in that room—everyone the soldiers had oppressed. But it quickly became evident that the people walking in circles, though they knew we were fighting to free them, made no effort to help in the fight because they wanted to appear neutral. They did not want to oppose the soldiers. As far as they were concerned, they were in a good place with the soldiers, and we were stirring up trouble. The soldiers weren't bothering them so long as they did what they were asked. They had gotten comfortable walking around in circles in a cage. So, not only were they not fighting with us, but they were getting in the way of our battle. They wouldn't move. They wouldn't advise when we couldn't see around them. They just became a huge stumbling block.

I looked around the room and saw that we were being annihilated. Man after man was falling at the hands of an armed soldier. Our numbers were down to almost nothing, and my last thought was at least we went down fighting. But then, something crazy happened. The doors opened and a blinding white light shown into the building. Out of the light, stepped in this army of warriors who looked like giants. They were not able to be penetrated by guns. They were unstoppable. They came in like a strong force, and they began to swoop up everyone who was fighting from under the hand of the oppressing soldiers. We knew we were saved by a heavenly army of angels. Suddenly, all the people walking around in circles lifted their heads with gladness. You could see the relief on their faces. "Yes, we are being saved." They began raising their hands at the angels so that the angels would not miss them, but the angels looked right pass them, only gathering those who had been in the fight. After the angels had collected their last fighting man, they shut the doors back on the masked soldiers and on the people walking in circles to remain right where they were. The people taken up by the angels were not being taken to sit. They were being taken to forcefully advance the Kingdom of God with the army of the Lord.

So where does Mrs. Jones fit? Mrs. Jones was one of the people walking in circles. She was one of those who thought, "Surely, I will be saved because I stayed neutral. I did what kept me safe. Surely God understands." The interpretation was quite clear to me. Mrs. Jones represented believers who have decided to play it safe instead of righteously standing and fighting for all things God. They decided to please people and their leaders rather than to grow and advance according to the will of God for their lives. They got the acceptance they wanted from man, but they didn't become close to anything that God had ordained them to become. They never became because they counted the costs to themselves as being too great. They sought comfort. They sought pleasure. They sought familiarity. They sought after their own safety and security of the flesh and, therefore, they missed the safety and security of the Lord.

At the end of this dream, the Lord said, "I am separating the wheat from the tares," and I quickly understood that the tares were not simply wicked unbelievers, they were believers who refused to do the will of God when He asked because it made them uncomfortable. And this made them useless in the army of the Lord. One thing I'd hate to become is useless to God.

In the waking world, Mrs. Jones was doing her active duty as a believer. In the eyes of God, Mrs. Jones was in the way of the true believer. In the waking world, Mrs. Jones was everything her ministry needed her to be. In the eyes of God, she was unwilling to be everything God needed her to be. In the waking world, Mrs. Jones's leaders were leading according to the heart of the Father. In the eyes of God, Mrs. Jones's leaders were leading according to their own hearts, causing the people of God to live in oppression.

Through one dream, God told His truth. Just as He did with Pilot's wife. Despite the story that the Pharisees were giving concerning the "crimes" of Jesus, God made it clear to Pilot's wife, through a dream, that Jesus was innocent. What she was hearing and seeing in the waking world was not the true perspective even if the majority was saying that it was.

In every one of these instances, in one way or another, the dream was used to bring light to the dark. Whether the dark represented an uncertain godly purpose, an unknown action, a misread situation, a falsified outlook, or a wrong point of focus, the dream brought truth to them all. We must come to a place as a body where we can see the power of the dream for what it truly is to God. What is the dream to God? It is one of God's most powerful methods for delivering truth, especially when it comes with the power of accurate interpretation.

# CHAPTER FIVE

# ACCURATE INTERPRETATION— DREAMSMEN'S SECOND SUPERPOWER

Stronger than Dreamsmen's power to dream is their ability to interpret the dream. How powerful would Iron Man's suit be without a strong interpretation or understanding for how each part is to be used? Look at the story below:

> A farmer went out to sow his seed. As he was scattering the seed, some fell along the path, and the birds came and ate it up. Some fell on rocky places, where it did not have much soil. It sprang up quickly, because the soil was shallow. But when the sun came up, the plants were scorched, and they withered because they had no root. Other seed fell among thorns, which grew up and choked the plants so that they did not bear grain. Still other seed fell on good soil. It came up, grew and produced a crop, some multiplying thirty, some sixty, some a hundred times.

Believe it or not, this story is taken straight out of the Bible (Mark 4:3–8). It was one of Jesus's many parables. At first glance, any person who hears this story would hear just another story, but look how powerful it becomes with the power of interpretation:

| The Parable of the Sower | |
| --- | --- |
| **Symbols** | **Interpretation** |
| The seed | The message about the kingdom, the word of God, the Lord's instruction, the promise of the Lord |
| The path where birds ate it up | Satan, or the enemy (birds), snatches or eats up the message, word, instruction, or promise from the people who have it but gets no understanding about it once he receives it. |
| Rocky places with not very much soil | People who receive "the seed" with joy, but . . . |
| Springs quickly, but when the sun comes up, plants become scorched and wither away because they have no root. | Since "the seed" has no root in the rocky places (people), when trouble comes (the scorching sun), the people quickly fall away. |
| Thorns that grew up and choked the plants | People who hear the word, act on the word, and begin to see some form of evidence of the word, but the worries of life and the deceitfulness of wealth choke the word and make the word unfruitful. |
| Good soil | People who hear the word and understand it |
| The 100, 60, 30 crop return | The return for everything sown into the kingdom, and everything it costs you to serve in the kingdom |

This story begins to show itself in our lives; we can look on and identify how this story applies itself in our lives. We can begin to make the personal adjustments necessary to see to it that the choices we make, our everyday actions, are aligning us with a 100-fold crop return. Whether we are worrying ourselves out of the word becomes something we need to evaluate. Are we getting understanding about the word? The interpretation of the story or parable gives us power to change to produce promise.

Dreams like some of those shared in the previous chapter are quite literal; that is, the dream implies exactly what the dreamer sees that it applies. For example, when God told Abraham in a dream that Sarah would have a son, the dream literally meant that Sarah would have a son. There was nothing hidden in the dream to be discovered. On the other hand, some dreams are not literal but are full of symbolism to enforce a point or a message much like the parable above. The power then, in cases like these, comes from the interpretation.

The powerful thing about interpretation of a dream is that it is very difficult for anyone to dispute. Why? Because 10 times out of 10, the symbols are so intelligently chosen and remarkably organized that the interpretation comes across as such an intellectually advanced summarization beyond anything the human mind could produce alone. There is such an accuracy that accompanies the dream interpretation that is almost inconceivable. We are capable of great things, but some things we would never be able to conceptualize in our own minds.

Sometimes to enforce the source of the dream and the validity of the interpretation, God will leave the dreaming to be done only through the person that the dream is for, and He gives the interpretation to skilled Dreamsmen. It becomes the responsibility of the person dreaming the dream to then seek out the Dreamsmen for the interpretation, but this is not the standard practice of the church today.

If we begin experiencing chest pains, shortness of breath, or anything of the sort, we exercise standard procedures to see a doctor who specializes in diagnosing our symptoms. We understand enough to know that whatever we are experiencing requires someone capable of telling us what it means, so that we know what we need to do to fix it. We do this because our life is important to us. Yet we don't place the same value on a dream. If we have an impressionable dream, something out of the ordinary that leaves us uneasy, uncomfortable, fearful, or with so many questions, we either take the chance of "diagnosing" it on our own without seeking the "professional help" of a Dreamsmen, or we don't bother to diagnose it at all. "Oh well, it was just a dream," we say. And we neglect to acknowledge what the dream *really* stands for. So what you are really saying is, "Oh well, it was just a message from God to ensure my purpose-filled life," or "Oh well, it was just a warning to prevent me from making costly decisions," or "Oh well, it was just something God needed me to see His way."

A dream is the symptom; the interpretation is the diagnosis that leads to proper treatment of the symptom. In the same way that Dreamsmen need to understand that through the divine power of interpretation they are extremely vital vessels for implementing godly treatment to worldly systems all over the land, believers need to strongly acknowledge the need for the Dreamsmen's interpretation and act accordingly.

Let me bring your attention to the book of Daniel, chapter 2. The king had a dream, and he immediately acknowledged the need to interpret it. His issue was locating a Dreamsmen who could interpret for him. The dream by itself was meaningless. The king had access to the very best in the land to assist him with the interpretation, but the men with their great skills and abilities were not of any assistance to the king. I imagine they must have been gifted in some magnificent way; otherwise, they would not have been considered for such a task. The king became so outraged that he ordered everyone to be killed if his dream wasn't interpreted. So, Daniel, a biblical Dreamsmen, sought God for the dream itself with its divine interpretation.

## The King's Dream

*Arioch took Daniel to the king at once and said, "I have found a man among the exiles from Judah who can tell the king what his dream means." The king asked Daniel (also called Belteshazzar), "Are you able to tell me what I saw in my dream and interpret it?" Daniel replied, "No wise man, enchanter, magician or diviner can explain to the king the mystery he has asked about, but there is a God in heaven who reveals mysteries. He has shown King Nebuchadnezzar what will happen in days to come. Your dream and the visions that passed through your mind as you were lying in bed are these: As Your Majesty was lying there, your mind turned to things to come, and the revealer of mysteries showed you what is going to happen. As for me, this mystery has been revealed to me, not because I have greater wisdom than anyone else alive, but so that Your Majesty may know the interpretation and that you may understand what went through your mind. Your Majesty looked, and there before you stood a large statue—an enormous, dazzling statue, awesome in appearance. The head of the statue was made of pure gold, its chest and arms of silver, its belly and thighs of bronze, its legs of iron, its feet partly of iron and partly of baked clay. While you were watching, a rock was cut out, but not by human hands. It struck the statue on its feet of iron and clay and smashed them. Then the iron, the clay, the bronze, the silver and the gold were all broken to pieces and became like chaff on a threshing floor in the summer. The wind swept them away without leaving a trace. But the rock that struck the statue became a huge mountain and filled the whole earth."*

—Dan. 2:25–35

What follows is a Dreamsmen's interpretation of the king's dream as God gave the interpretation through Daniel:

*This was the dream, and now we will interpret it to the king. Your Majesty, you are the king of kings. The God of heaven has given you dominion and power and might and glory; in your hands he has placed all mankind and the beasts of the field and the birds in the sky. Wherever they live, he has made you ruler over them all. You are that head of gold. After you, another kingdom will arise, inferior to yours. Next, a third kingdom, one of bronze, will rule over the whole earth. Finally, there will be a fourth kingdom, strong as iron—for iron breaks and smashes everything— and as iron breaks things to pieces, so it will crush and break all the others. Just as you saw that the feet and toes were partly of baked clay and partly of iron, so this will be a divided kingdom; yet it will have some of the strength of iron in it, even as you saw iron mixed with clay. As the toes were partly iron and partly clay, so this kingdom will be partly strong and partly brittle. And just as you saw the iron mixed with baked clay, so the people will be a mixture and will not remain united, any more than iron mixes with clay. In the time of those kings, the God of heaven will set up a kingdom that will never be destroyed, nor will it be left to another people. It will crush all those kingdoms and bring them to an end, but it will itself endure forever. This is the meaning of the vision of the rock cut out of a mountain, but not by human hands—a rock that broke the iron, the bronze, the clay, the silver and the gold to pieces. The great God has shown the king what will take place in the future. The dream is true and its interpretation is trustworthy.*

—Dan. 2:36–45

What we must not fail to see is that the interpretation that accompanies the dream is not just the luck of the draw. Interpretation isn't the average human skill that is learned like reading. It is something uniquely portioned to specific people so that God can continue to exercise His will in the land.

In our day, we have dream sites all over the web where you can type in symbols or words to understand the significance of them in a dream. These dream sites are much like the magicians, enchanters, sorcerers, and astrologers the king had handy to consult for hidden meanings. They have many answers and knowledge of things unknown, and they are there for people to easily gather information, but their knowledge base is not enough to convey or reveal the mysteries of God. As Daniel did, Dreamsmen search out dream meanings in a different way. While there may be some common meanings among some of these search engines, the full interpretation will never come from them alone. God does this intentionally just to make it known at all times that he is the giver of dreams and the one true interpreter of the dreams He gives. Daniel had no search engines. He had no interpretation manuals. All he had was God who had given the dream, and by His power, Daniel was given the ability to interpret it in a way no one else could.

Dreamsmen will not pull their meaning from search engines; instead, they will seek first the mind and heart of God. While I have made myself familiar with dream symbolism through the web and books, I never look to find God's interpretation of a dream in them unless directed, and I am very rarely directed there at this point in my life. I have found that God is His own dictionary with His own set of symbols and His own set of meanings for His own specific times. Today, I may see a lion in my dream, and it is symbolic of the Lion of Judah. Tomorrow, I may see a lion in my dream, and it serves as a warning to be on the alert. My point is that the interpretation is God's, not man's. It has been over two years since I've used any dream website to understand a God-given dream because I have learned where the power of my interpretation comes from and how to trust in the source of that power. Part of my hesitation in the past was not understanding the interpretation power within me. That is, the power of interpretation that comes with being built up a Dreamsmen.

Allow me to give you a real dream example. Some years ago, I had a dream that I was sitting in a room with individuals having a meeting. As we all began to exit out of the meeting room, I had plans or blueprints in one hand, which I imagined was developed as a direct result of what was discussed in the meeting, and my wallet in my other hand. When we got outside, my attention was immediately captured by a huge net that had suddenly fallen from the sky. The net was enormous, and it was dangling from what appeared to be a humongous plane hovering in the sky. For some reason my first instinct told me to take all my stuff and climb the net.

As I began trying to figure out a plan to climb this net with full hands, I distinctly noticed that I was wearing purple heels. It was clear to me this was not going to be an easy climb. I had plans in one hand, my wallet in the other hand, and purple heels on my feet to climb in. So, I did what any normal person would do. I tried to find innovative ways to make this climb happen. I rolled up the plans and placed them under one arm, and I placed my wallet under the other arm. I tightened my arms enough to hold what was under my arms securely, and I began climbing up with two free hands.

As I was making the climb and was about halfway up the net, my wallet escaped me. I watched in despair as it fell all the way down. I thought, "Oh my God, I am going to have to go all the way back down to get it. This can't be good." As I stood there trying to figure out my next move, someone who was climbing the net below me shouted out, "I caught your wallet." And they tossed the wallet back up to me. So once again, I placed the wallet back under my arm and continued to climb.

Finally, I could see the plane, and I could see the mounting platform to get on the plane. I quickly tossed my wallet, the plans, everything I had onto the mounting platform above me, so that I had both my arms and hands to pull myself up onto the platform. What happened next placed me in a panic. Everything I had tossed up slid off the other side of the platform and fell all the way down to ground. I was so high up at this point that I could no longer see the ground. I wondered what I was supposed to do. Was I to go all the way back down and get my things? But then the answer to that question quickly became clear as I realized that the plane was ready for takeoff. I was very aware that if I did not get on this plane right then, I would miss its departure and with that the final destination. I made the choice to board the plane and leave the plans and wallet behind. Once I boarded the plane, the doors shut, and the plane transformed into a bus and took off into the air. That concluded my dream.

With so much symbolism and so much taking place in this dream, I knew there was clearly something God wanted me to understand about it. So, I sought the Holy Spirit for meaning. And by seeking the Holy Spirit first for the meaning, I was given the following interpretation: The net was symbolic in itself of a fisher's net. God, our heavenly Father had cast His net to round up those He was calling to become His next assigned group of fishers of men. This was symbolic of the moment when Jesus was rounding up each of His disciples one by one to make them ready for what they would be called to do. The net was abruptly dropped from the sky because what God would be calling us to do would literally abruptly interrupt our lives and the things we thought we had going on, just as Jesus had interrupted the lives of His chosen disciples. We would then have to make a choice to either drop and climb or ignore the net and follow after our own wills.

The purple heels I took notice of in the dream symbolized our call and acceptance to be God's "Royal Priesthood" as we embark on the uncomfortable journey that accepting this climb would lead us into. The plans were symbolic of all the plans we think are important to the climb, and the wallet was symbolic of our old identity or everything with which we once identified. This dream was boldly stating that the main requirement for this next level of assignment is for us to lose the old self and everything we thought we needed to be ourselves. With this assignment came a new identity and a new plan. We could not get on the plane and into the next assignment holding on to everything that we thought we were and everything that was.

There was a point in the dream when a woman farther down below me tried to throw the fallen wallet back up to me. That meant that those behind us will only know us as we were, and if we let them, they will keep us functioning as we were. However, if we keep climbing, we will come into fellowship and covenant relationship with people who will know us as we are according to God's perspective and perfect will. But to get to them, we must get onto the plane, and the climb onto the plane definitely comes with a time stamp.

Finally, what we think should happen instantly just because we said yes will take time and will require patience. This was indicated by the transformation of the plane into a bus. We got onto the plane, but we have to trust the process of getting to the final destination. Of course, there were other key elements to take notice of such as how trying to keep your identity (the wallet and plans) made the climb that much harder and that much more longer, but in a nutshell, God was saying, "The time has come, lose yourself, and follow Me, up into the next level of assignment that I have purposed for you."

I shared this dream with you to point out one simple fact: this interpretation did not derive from a dream book or a dream website. The interpretation of this dream came from God by way of the Holy Spirit, and it was used to preach and teach a message of the Lord. Some of my most powerful sermons are driven and centered on the symbolic dreams given to me by God through interpretation. Just as Jesus did with the parables, God still does today through dreams and dream interpretation. Jesus said let those who have ears to hear, hear. We have to ask ourselves, "Have we given ourselves the ears to hear, or have we shut down before the release of the interpretation?" There is a Daniel for every dream, but we have to respect the power of the dream enough to seek after the Daniel or the Dreamsmen for the Interpretation, even if the Dreamsmen is you. The truth is, we live in a world where the power of the interpretation frightens us because it exposes us, challenges us, and oftentimes reroutes us. As a result, it makes being Dreamsmen one of the most difficult roles to walk in, especially when they are exposing, challenging, and rerouting a Jezebel.

# CHAPTER SIX

## BECOMING AN ENDGAME SUPERHERO FOR JEZEBEL

What are superheroes really? Are they real? Are they really that uncommon? According to the *Merriam-Webster* dictionary, superheroes are defined two ways:

- "A fictional hero having extraordinary or superhuman powers"
- "An exceptionally skillful or successful person"

Let's take a moment to look deeper into the definitions. The first uses the words *fictional*, *extraordinary*, and *superhuman*. From this perspective, Spider-Man, Captain America, Thor, Wonder Woman, and Aquaman are all considered superheroes. They are fictional characters who have extraordinary and/or superhuman powers. I mean, what average human can call thunder and lightning from the sky? This is not your average everyday power. Yet, biblically speaking, there were individuals who operated in extraordinary superhuman powers. No one pulled thunder and lightning from the sky, but Elijah did call fire down from heaven. No average man is walking around with super-strength or super-speed, but biblically speaking, Elijah ran with the chariot, and Samson had strength beyond any most humans.

The second definition uses the words *exceptionally skillful* and *successful*. Again, biblically speaking, David was an exceptionally skillful warrior who never lost a battle. David's, Elijah's, and Samson's "superhero" strengths were all used to stand against and bring down real Bible villains. So now I ask, would God stop now? Biblical history has demonstrated that for every villain or captive situation that rears its ugly face in the presence of God's people, God has a superhero waiting in the wings who, by the power of the Holy Spirit, operates beyond the power of any man to bring down diabolical systems that keep people in bondage and to enforce the changes that God wishes to see. Samson had incredibly noteworthy strength that appeared to be greater than the strength of any other man in his time. God used Samson's strength to fulfill His word and end the lives of all the Philistines. Then there's Moses, who God endowed with miracle-working power to perform works that would eventually lead to the release of an entire nation of Israelites from the Egyptian army. So, if there is indeed a Jezebel still operating in the land and posing a threat to the people of God whether they recognize it or not, then rest assured that God has some real-life superheroes ready to make their stand.

Real-life, holy, spirit-filled superheroes existed then, and they still very much exist today. Unfortunately, several reasons keep the body of Christ and the world from experiencing these supernatural hero occurrences as we should today. Some of these include:

1. People do not know they possess the superhuman spiritually endowed gifts.
2. People recognize that a spiritual gift exists, but they are too afraid and/or have too little knowledge about it to know or experience its depth.
3. People do not understand that they are an answer to something God has identified as a problem, or they do not know what problem they are the answer to.

4. There's not a lot of accessible training, or too little time is spent learning and exercising the superhuman spiritually endowed gifts to their full potential.

5. Superhuman spiritually endowed gifts come with a greater cost that many aren't prepared to pay.

6. People choose how they want their gifts to be used as opposed to how God wants to use them.

Finally, all six of the reasons listed above can be credited to what I have identified as reason number 7. That is, the ruling and controlling powers of Jezebel are lurking within the body of Christ and strategically working to keep people living ignorantly in bondage as she discredits, traps, hides away, or sends out orders to kill true superhero gifts— specifically when they are coming into an ounce of knowledge of who they are meant to be and what they are purposed to do.

Imagine the moment when Moses first realized his power to access God at a level uncanny to man. Imagine then, what he must have felt when he realized what God wanted to do with him through this power and the magnitude of the problem he was to solve. Imagine how Moses felt when he was starting to understand the gift he had and the position it would place him in. Moses did not find out about his gift in a classroom full of students talking about the commonality of superhuman spiritually endowed gifts. Moses was not entered into a "Superhuman Draft" in which he sat among people just like him who had been training all this time for the moment to be chosen to do what they were most skilled to do. His gift was emerging at a time when no one would really care for it because of the changes and discomfort it would bring when he fully accessed it. His gift was developing at a time when Pharaoh's system of doing things was already fully established as the way. How do you accept that what has been is going to be challenged by you through gifts you don't fully understand?

This is that moment in the movies when the fictional superhero realizes what he can do and how that is intended to make great good in the world. This is the moment the fictional superhero has to decide whether to suppress the powers and pretend they aren't there or become expert in the powers to do the good they were intended for, even though there is little backing or support for them. I can safely assume that there is a lot of fear involved in this moment because the person does not know how others will perceive this power, or what they will do when it is revealed to the world that this kind of unconventional power resides in them.

After being bitten by a spider, Spider-Man realized that he had special abilities to conquer an evil that had become prevalent in his community. He also realized that his life would never be the same because of his special abilities, and in an effort to maintain some kind of a normal life, he chooses to hide his identity. Why? Because an emerging superhero will always be the target of attack when what they are emerging for interrupts somebody's already established system. Just like other emerging heroes in the world of fiction, the very gifts that Moses had been given placed him in direct opposition with the established leadership and their system. More plainly stated, Moses's very Spirit-endowed power or gifts made him a primary target for a Jezebel spirit wanting nothing more than to discredit everything Moses was and everything Moses stood for. This is also a 21st-century Dreamsmen's experience. This was my experience.

The challenge for an emerging Dreamsmen is that they are usually emerging at the time of Jezebel's reign. Consequently, once they begin to disclose their power, the attacks to discredit, trap, or destroy them begin immediately. Allow me to make this plain for just a moment.

I had a dream once in which I saw church leaders and Pastors in a church holding people in bondage by misplacing them in assignments ordered by man, then giving them recognition and praise in the misplaced assignments so that the people would never move into the assignments God had called them to. In my dream, one young woman was being awarded a visual art award and she by no means drew, painted, or did anything artsy. She knew it was strange. She knew it interfered with what she needed to be doing, but the recognition appeased her. It drew her, and she chose to take up her award and stay misplaced. Several people were intentionally being misplaced, then awarded for what I will refer to as "decoy assignments" to benefit the Pastors' vision, not God's. As a result, the people were doing nothing, nor were they growing in the assignments God called them into. The public recognition was simply a deceptive tactic being implemented to manipulate the people into remaining in a place of stagnation, and it was happening in the church.

A very difficult truth that the body of Christ needs to face is that the church is becoming a place for people to become comfortable with not becoming at all. That is, never becoming all God has called them to be. In other words, Jezebel or the spirit of Jezebel, whose primary mission is to maintain her control by keeping in chains the fullness of God's work, has made a secure hiding place in the church. Remember, from Chapter 3: (1) Jezebel wants control; (2) Jezebel wants all the power; (3) Jezebel hides behind a show; (4) Jezebel leads you into bondage or captivity, stagnating you from purpose; (5) Jezebel makes false accusations to kill the gift; (6) Jezebel is religious; and (7) Jezebel seeks to tie you down with traditional practices and religious works. In the preceding dream, the spirit of Jezebel was in full operation in the church manipulating people to stay stuck in bondage by making them feel good in not doing. But God is infiltrating these systems with an answer. Repeating what was once written by Chuck Pierce, "The Holy Spirit is now restoring the power of the night watch in the Church."[1]

Dreamsmen have emerged and are emerging to expose, correct, and call to order dysfunctional, diabolical, and deceptive systems in the body of Christ or in the church. However, these systems are strategically disguised and have remained hidden for years behind religion and tradition, making it that much more difficult for the already established leaders to

---

1. Chuck Pierce, Foreword to *Dream Language: The Prophetic Power of Dreams, Revelations, and the Spirit of Wisdom*, James W. Goll and Michal A. Goll (Shippensburg, PA: Destiny Image Publishers Inc, 2006), 14.

accept or admit that these systems are indeed dysfunctional, diabolical, and deceptive in the sight of God. So when an emerging Dreamsmen, who is the acting minority, steps onto the scene where these systems have been ruling and operating under ministerial authorities for extensive periods of time, the Dreamsmen and the gift usually come under attack when they begin to reveal what has been disclosed to them by God as being a travesty. And unlike Spider-Man, their identify is not concealed.

Can I go back to Chapter 2 for a moment? Remember the ways in which Jezebel attacked her challengers. In the case of Naboth, she used religion, traditional practices, and manipulation to disguise the attack that discredited Naboth and had him killed. In the case of Elijah, she drove him into hiding and nudged him into a state in which he wanted to put the gifts down. It is challenging for a Dreamsmen to become because the very recognition or use of their gift through which they often become makes their whole process of emergence a target of attack.

A Dreamsmen's gift is not necessarily nurtured or watered by the church. In fact, it is more likely to be feared and misunderstood by the church. Why? Because a Dreamsmen gives God's perspective, no matter who or what it implicates, and oftentimes, it is God's perspective that becomes the missing part as leaders do whatever it takes to keep their churches operational. Remember, Jezebel didn't think her way of life was evil, no more than many Bishops, Pastors, and ministerial leaders believe that their way of operating their churches or ministries is evil in the eyes of God. But pride and ego kept Jezebel blind while humility and love opened Paul's eyes to truth. Unfortunately, there are many leaders choosing to stay blind because of the perceived "losses" they think will come with the acceptance of God's change.

At a time when Dreamsmen are crucial for the rise of the church and at a time when dreams are becoming a major form of heavenly communication, the body of Christ under the influence of Jezebel is choosing to downplay them, casting them off as nothing more than a human thought, a subconscious feeling, a devilish download, or the aftereffect of something seen, experienced, or eaten. Even though God makes it clear that in the last days dreams will be a major form of communication, the body of Christ at large remains uneducated about the significance of the dream and the Dreamsmen. So, it becomes a real struggle for Dreamsmen to emerge when there is nothing in place that is teaching, building, or supporting everything a Dreamsmen is. In fact, not very many churches prepare their congregations to even acknowledge the dreamer as a messenger of God. In the body of Christ, dreams are almost always seen as taboo. James Goll, the coauthor of *Dream Language*, states:

> Many people today, particularly in the Western culture, never recognize God speaking to them in this way because they have been conditioned by a skeptical and sophisticated society to discount the language of dreams. Unfortunately, this includes many Christian believers also.[2]

So, what does a Dreamsmen do? In a church world controlled by the spirit of Jezebel, how does a Dreamsmen become without doubting his process? That is the challenge of a Dreamsmen. And it is a real challenge. Because again, they are dreaming things and seeing things that lead to paradigm shifts not visible to the waking or natural eye. James Goll so eloquently points out how the birth of Israel was first spoken of through a dream given to Abraham as he slept on the desert sands.

Through the dream, I have seen a well-respected Bishop leading a prominent church dressed in drag, acting like a woman as he preaches the word of God against such things. I have seen a minister leading a wonderful kingdom ministry secretly cheating on his wife. I have seen leaders who were supposed to be elevated looked over because they were not a popular or renowned voice. Yet, they were the voice that would

2. James W. Goll and Michal A. Goll, *Dream Language: The Prophetic Power of Dreams, Revelations, and the Spirit of Wisdom* (Shippensburg, PA: Destiny Image Publishers Inc, 2006), 20.

positively and influentially change everything for the future of the assembly given the platform to do so. I have seen ministries operating in ungodly cycles because of what the leaders refused to see. I have seen the real motives behind "kingdom relationships exposed." I have seen sickness and death on people who look perfectly healthy because of a secretive life of sin they had been engaged in for years. And these are to expose a few. Do you think that the church is really ready to acknowledge and accept the emergence and the power of Dreamsmen? Do you think the church is truly ready to acknowledge the power of a dream? Twice I've had church leaders refuse to even hear a dream when the dream provided direction to their purpose. But I will discuss more of the why behind that later on in the book.

Funny thing, the becoming Dreamsmen has a better experience emerging in the secular world than in the body of Christ. I've had to reach out to people who are far from spiritual but who receive the dream with more gratitude and appreciation than those in leadership positions in the church. Why? Because Jezebel is most present in leadership—especially leadership in the body of Christ. This is why it is important that a Dreamsmen not come out on the church scene with the gift prematurely before God has had time to secretly establish him or her. Pastors and church leaders do not happily and willingly accept orders, truth, and awakenings that come from God through a Dreamsmen, especially when it is exposing errors, mandating correction, or forcing change from what has always been. On the contrary, Jezebel is ready to tear a Dreamsmen down using this very common language against them: "wild, uncontrollable, challenging, troublemaker, unsubmissive, divisive, misguided in the word and the interpretation, liar, and too deep." What words do you think Pharaoh might have used to describe Moses? After all, Pharaoh had only been executing the same system that had been established for years. Do you really think that Pharaoh saw himself as the troublemaker?

I'd like to end this chapter by sharing a dream experience I had with an established leader in the church. Both the leader and I were very confident and very certain God was setting her up for a great move that would position her for a greater level in her assigned work. I loved this leader and absolutely wanted God's absolute best for her. She had gone through so much. She had taken multiple hits and had multiple losses. So just to witness a turn of events for her would be an understatement. We wanted to see heaven just rain the glory down on everything she put her hands to, and we wanted to see what this great new transition would have in store for her.

She had a few things going on to position her for this great move, but then something else happened. A job offer that wasn't initially a part of the established plans was presented to her. At first glance, I was happy for her. I mean, it too would place her where she truly felt she needed to be for the work God had assigned to her to truly commence. So I celebrated her. Then, came the dream that would change everything.

In the dream, I was traveling with her to her new job for her to finalize some paperwork. Once we got there, we were escorted by a woman who sat both of us down and began to confirm previous interview statements that had been given by the transitioning leader. As she began to go through the questions and answers, it became clear to me that had the leader given the answers God had previously exposed to her about her assignment, she would not have been the chosen candidate for this job. Because I was in the room and she knew that I knew the answers she should have given, she began to clean the previous answers up a bit to match what she and I both knew the answer should have been. Of course, now this caused a bit of confusion for the woman handling the paperwork.

The woman asking all the questions looked in my direction and said, "With the answers you are giving me now, this is not the job you are supposed to be doing. In fact, you need to be seeking something closer to what you are speaking to." Then she paused and said, "But we've already hired you. So at this point we just have to make it work." Then she dismissed us to another room where the transitioning leader had to complete a medical exam. Both her blood pressure and her kidneys were well and at the best they had been. And despite what had happened in the previous room, we both got excited about that. Then the medical examiner began to look into her womb. His whole demeanor changed at this point. He revealed that she had been carrying a fetus, but it had died. And the reason for its death was that her entire womb was filled with old brown blood. He went on to say, "If we don't fix this, you will be barren and nothing more will be able to birth from you." So he encouraged her to stop and have this addressed. I then cosigned with the medical examiner and said, "This is why you have been barren this long. Let's just deal with this so that you can finally deliver your babies." The transitioning leader looked at me and told me, "It's fine. I don't want to miss this opportunity, so I'm not going to worry about it." The medical examiner and I looked at each other in distress, realizing she was not seeing the severity of what was being shown to her and what it could mean if she ignored this information and moved on with the job. She literally walked out the room and kept the process moving.

When I woke up, God made it clear to me that the new job was not His will for her and that something had already died the moment she made the choice to take it. He also disclosed to me that in working that job, she wouldn't be able to produce any fruit from her womb. In addition, there was too much old/bad blood still floating in her that needed to be addressed and cleaned out before her life could really produce at the level it was intended.

I honestly hated the fact that I had this dream when I wanted so badly for this to be the final turnaround for her. I mean I absolutely hated it. I even tried to revisit the dream countless times to search out an alternative meaning that I might have overlooked. I did not want to have to tell this leader, my friend, that what she thought was an open door from God was destructive to her God-given assignment. But I did. I mustered up the courage and shared the dream with her along with the interpretation given to me.

What took place after is a Dreamsmen's nightmare. She became very cold toward me, and I became the villain. She stopped speaking to me as if we were nothing and as if I no longer existed. All the great love she said she had for me and all the respect she had for God in me were gone in the blink of an eye because of a dream. Then, on top of everything, she disguised this ugly behavior with religion for those who would listen. This ministerial leader, who couldn't receive a Dreamsmen's dream because of the perceived "loss" she'd have to take labeled me the "troublemaker" and only because I told her the dream.

Can I go back to the movie *Captain America: Civil War*? The Avengers become the villain not because they are doing something wrong but because they are using their power to do something right. But their righteous actions bring discomfort to the land because they don't bring the results that the powers that be think they should. Keep in mind, however, that the powers that be feel they are doing what's in the best interest of the people. The final result is that a handful of Avengers are forced into hiding or exile with a price on their heads for their capture and return. And the truth is, for a moment, after that response—after that turn—I wanted to distance myself from any further assignments to protect myself from feeling this kind of hurt ever again.

The emergence of a Dreamsmen is a hurtful process, especially when it challenges the very will or desire of another. False accusation, loneliness, betrayal, exile, second- and third-guessing about the gifts and the revelations, being misunderstood, target practice, and more become a part of the emerging process. If a Dreamsmen isn't careful, a surviving Jezebel spirit within the church can literally wipe him or her out before the Dreamsmen's full emergence is complete. This you will see in the next chapter, but before you read any further, please allow me to emphasize this point:

> Nothing that has been stated thus far or that will be stated in the chapters ahead has been written to discredit or condemn the church or the leaders within it. Rather it is to expose the church to the church so that with new

knowledge, education, and God-given understanding, we can correct what has been and become what we, the church, should be. It is to no one's benefit to drown a Dreamsmen out or overlook a Dreamsmen's dream no matter how hard the implication of the dream, no matter your knowledge and/or experience over the Dreamsmen who shared it, and no matter your opinion of the Dreamsmen sent to you. God gave the body gifts, and all these gifts are necessary for the full functioning of God's people. Let us soften our hearts and receive this message and the message of the Dream so that God may give us full clarity to purposefully and prosperously grow.

# CHAPTER SEVEN

# "IN THE CHURCH RING"–LOSS OF A DREAMSMEN

My father, Reverend Cornell Bethel, sat alone in front of every church leader, including their wives, having been refused by the same leadership the presence of his very own wife. With the Pastor, six reverends, eight other ministers, ten deacons, other leaders, and their wives, my father was ordered to stare shame, false accusation, judgment, lies, betrayal, and pain in the eyes of the same leaders with whom he had faithfully served, preached, fellowshipped, and ministered.

How did it get to that point? How was it that just a month prior, Reverend Cornell Bethel was successfully leading an outreach ministry that was thriving in the Miami communities, but now he was here. The outreach ministry fed, clothed, and saved the lives of so many people. I can recall as a child going to impoverished communities in vans and trucks and being swarmed by masses of people as my father led his team into meeting the needs of these people. I recall walking into a warehouse so organized and set up with hundreds of clothes, shoes, and items that would assist so many. People anticipated this team. They anticipated my father, and the work was so fruitful and publicly noticeable that there was nothing he could ask for that his Pastor would deny him. Whatever he needed from his leader, he received because he did his work well. But now the keys to the warehouse were snatched, the position my father walked in was stripped, and the keys that gave my father access to the church were taken away. Now he faced an endless cycle of meetings that would make him the object of humiliation and identify him as public church enemy number one. How did it get here? The answer is simple. My father had a dream.

One morning, my father woke up terrified, shaken, and completely stirred. He turned to his wife, my mother, to tell her, "I was in hell." He went on to describe in great detail what he had just experienced in the dream. He shared that it was not just him in hell, but that it was the entire church, and the entire church ignorantly and blindly followed its Pastor, the leader at that time, right into the doors of hell. In fact, the church had been so blinded that even as they entered hell, they were still fully unaware of what was taking place around them. My father pointed out that he could see Satan on the throne and quickly arrived at the conclusion that "there is no getting out. We are all in hell." Suddenly, the Pastor was no longer standing with them. He had been taken to another room where he was being subjected to another level of endless torment. The church was in hell, and my father sat helplessly as he watched everyone walk straight in. But he could not forget the factor that would terrify him the most. He was right there with them. When he had finally been released to wake up from this terrifying dream, he knew exactly what it meant and what needed to be done, and he knew he had to do it.

You see, as stated above, my father would receive anything that he asked for or needed to run his ministry as successfully as he did. Financially, there was nothing he would not get. But this too came with a price. My father bore witness to many wrongs being done inside the church. The systems were corrupt, and no matter the outside appearance, what was happening on the inside was wickedly tainted. Of course before the dream, my father chose to turn a blind eye because if he chose to shine light on what was being done in the dark, he knew it could affect his access and the good thing he had going with his ministry division. Consequently, Daddy chose to compromise, and this was the decision he would stick to until the dream.

After the dream he saw the real cost of compromise. He saw what being silent could mean for him and for the entire church. He knew at this point and he said to my mother, "I got to say something. I can't continue like this anymore." My father was making the choice to do what he had been ordered by the Lord so that what he saw and experienced for the church and himself would not be the final result. So Daddy talked.

My father was very close with his reverend buddies. They were truly a tight-knit family. I remember some of them hanging at our home or at one another's homes. So, surely, there was safety sharing with the other leaders. They knew my father's heart was for God and for the work of the ministry. But my father would quickly come to find out that was not at all the case. From the moment he released this dream, all except for one began to turn on him. The other reverends and ministers fired back a conclusion that Reverend Cornell Bethel placed the whole church in hell because "he" didn't like the way they systematically did things. Furthermore, they accused my father of intentionally casting judgment on the church and of planting wicked seeds among others within the church to cause division and other trouble. What my father believed to be his safety net became a launching pad for his removal, exile, and destruction.

Upon witnessing this sudden turn of events, my father wrote a confidential letter to his Pastor sharing the dream, explaining the interpretation given to him, disclosing some of the areas God would bring to his attention, and clarifying his intentions not to destroy, divide, or condemn the church, but to do his part in making sure the church was operating righteously and not failing to overlook areas in which God wanted to bring correction—especially given the intensity of the dream. He made it clear his love for God's work, the ministry, and his heart to see the church become all that God desires it to be, and he felt that this would bring the resolution necessary in such a chaotic situation. But he was wrong.

The Pastor received the letter, read the letter, and despite its confidential implication, made copies of the letter, called a meeting with every reverend, deacon, and minister in the church, and handed out a copy of the letter to every single one of them. That is, every leader except my father. And there was a logical reason why. The letter everyone received was not the letter my father had written. It was his letter minus an entire section. What section was that? It was the section that gave clarity. It was the section that spoke his heart for the church and his desire to do his part in the maintenance of righteous operations. It was the section that spoke to his love and desire to see the church be all that God desires it to be. It was the part that explained how the dream would be used to make the adjustments necessary so that the church would see the fruitful works of God executed righteously in the church. So, at this meeting the same angry reverends and ministers got together to once again speak to the so-called wicked actions taken against the church by my father who had condemned the whole church to hell.

After this meeting the keys to the warehouse, the keys to the church, and my father's removal from leadership and any work tied to it were so ordered. Just like that, the thriving outreach ministry had lost its leader. Another meeting was held after this. This meeting consisted of the Pastor and the whole outreach team. This meeting again did not include my father, but it included my father's wife, my mother. She sat as the Pastor explained why Reverend Cornell Bethel would no longer be leading the outreach ministry or leading in the church. Knowing what she knew and knowing the truth in its entirety, she grieved, as there was not even the hint of a dream mentioned. The reason my father was being removed now centered around false accusations and lies. No one was addressing the dream. A whole new case was built, and it was this fabricated case that would bring forth the hearing that placed my father alone in front of everyone without the presence of his wife.

The purpose of this hearing was to validate and justify the removal of Reverend Cornell Bethel as a leader in this ministry.

The hearing commenced and the accusations began, the betrayals were made clear, the people threw their stones, but in a room against over 20 people, my father took a Dreamsmen's stance, and at the end of it all, no fault could be found. The fabricated case could not hold, and in the end, the words that followed from the leadership side were, "Let's just forgive and forget," but the damage had been done. The heart was pierced. No one could go back to the way it was, and there was still the dream that no one wanted to acknowledge or accept. My father's keys were never handed back to him. His position was never given back to him.

This was the moment the body of Christ lost a Dreamsmen. This was the moment Elijah ran from Jezebel and told God he just didn't want to carry out the work anymore. This was the moment my father, Reverend Cornell Bethel, sank back into hiding and never came out. My father would never enter a church again, not as a leader, not as a member. He had been offered the opportunity to serve as a ministerial leader in other churches, but the answer was always no. He retreated into old habits. He lost his fire. The great community anointing he had would never be seen in full operation again. Right at that moment. He put down his work and never saw it to its completion. My father died at the age of 47.

Jezebel may have run Elijah into hiding, but Elijah ultimately made the choice to give up. What my father experienced because of his assignment as a Dreamsmen to share the dream was traumatizing indeed, but my father ultimately made the choice to give up, and I know this because he told me. Not in the waking world, but in a dream. About six or seven years after my father had passed and after I was well invested into a new life of ministry in the community, my father met me in a dream on a beach. I was sitting on pretty white sands, and my father came and met me to sit and advise me because of the path I would be called to take. He told me what pain his gift brought him. He told me I had the same gift and a very similar anointing for ministry.

And he told me I would encounter the same things. Then he told me, "Rachel, I made the wrong choice. I let what happened cause me to give up and not finish what I know I needed to do, but you can't do the same. You have to finish the work that I started, and when the gift puts you in the hot seat just keep going."

So you see, I do not blame the church for the choices we make, but I do see the importance of educating the church to what damages are caused when we make the conscious decision to make people a target because of what God discloses to them. I do see the need to expose the spirit of Jezebel in the church that feels challenged, threatened, and belittled every time a Dreamsmen steps on the scene with fresh revelation from God showing the need for systematic correction. A Dreamsmen is not coming for your position or for your church. A Dreamsmen is coming to see to it that God has His way in your position and in His church. God would much rather save His people than leave His people to die in deception. It benefits no one to make little of the dream. No one.

So, what's the final analysis? There are a couple of things that I want you to take away from this chapter. The first is the Dream. The dream exposed discontentment from God with the church's operations—not to permanently place the church in hell—but to make the church aware so that the necessary changes would be made to keep the church from experiencing what my father witnessed in his dream. My father, however, ran into a very common bump in the road. The leadership did not feel their systems were unrighteous. How could this be wrong? We are thriving. Things are going well. It's working well for everyone. This is where church leadership struggles. This is where Jezebel's head begins to rise, and leadership is flooded with all the wrong kinds of thoughts and assumptions. The thinking goes something like this:

> Receiving the dream means admitting we are wrong, and admitting we are wrong in front of someone less experienced could make us look incompetent. If we

appear to be incompetent, we could cause people not to want to follow us so that they begin following the one who exposed us. Even if there is something right in what they say, we cannot lose the confidence of the people or our control over the manner.

Another train of thought begins with the leadership feeling that their way is perfectly fine, and if God wants it changed, He'll change it. So the leader continues with what has been because nothing bad has surfaced from it thus far. No matter which train of thought is followed, Jezebel becomes the driving spirit behind refusal to change, unwillingness to admit, and too much pride to heed or listen.

Now, at the moment the leaders heard the dream from my father, they had a choice. They had the choice to do as Paul did—realize what they thought was right was wrong, have their vision repaired, and continue in the righteous way serving God. The other choice is to give in to their pride and their ego, relinquish full control to the spirit of Jezebel in hiding, wake it up, and become that church leader who goes into attack mode for anyone and anything that challenges their system. And again, not because they are evil, wicked people, but simply because they are holding on to what they perceive to be right.

Look at what followed my dad's submission to the dream when it would not be accepted: manipulation, deceit, lies, false accusations, and the congregated meetings behind closed doors to discredit him, and all of this was made to look justified. These are all tactics of a Jezebel spirit fully unleashed. My father became a threat to the systems already set, and it wasn't in anyone's agenda to see them changed.

Here's the part I want to fully bring to your attention. These were good spiritual people. I mentioned earlier that my father had awesome relationships with them. They knew the word. They did the work of the ministry wholeheartedly. They served diligently. But Jezebel doesn't need an evil person for her mission. She needs an influential person, a leader, who will hold tight to pride and ego when their own successful systems or own way of doing things is challenged. My father, the Dreamsmen, challenged their system, and the spirt of Jezebel was unleashed.

Jezebel lives, but only when leaders fail to humble themselves to the word and instruction of God, even when it seems contrary to what has always been. An ongoing fight still exists between Jezebel and the Prophets, but it is more disguised now than ever. Dreamsmen are necessary to end the fight, but the church must be willing to listen.

# CHAPTER EIGHT

# LIKE FATHER, LIKE DAUGHTER—BREAKING A FAMILY CYCLE

Another day was over. The night for me had come to an end. I could shut down, lie down, shut my eyes, and fall asleep. But the hours of sleep for me are not necessarily hours of sleep. No. It is in these moments some of my deepest revelations are given, the greatest mysteries from heaven are solved, instructions and insight are given, and directions to change the course of a person's life in an effort to position them for purpose are told. The latter was definitely the case this particular evening.

As I fell deeper into the dream state, the dream began. There I was, trying desperately to speak with my Pastor about several questions that I had. After much persistency, I was able to meet with my Pastor via the phone. Once I got him on the phone, I proceeded to ask him a series of questions. Then my Pastor responded to me and said, "I cannot answer any of those questions for you. That kind of knowledge and training I am unable to provide, but you will get the answers from John Eckhardt." The dream was over, and I woke up that morning with two very important revelations in my spirit. The first was the name John

Eckhardt. Who was that? Up until that moment, I had never heard that name before. The second was that my Pastor could not equip me with the skills, knowledge, and training I would need at this point to become whatever it was God would need me to become to fulfill my godly purpose. I had reached my peak at my current church, and it would take a new leader, a new covering to take me into my next. But was it John Eckhart?

I thought so. I thought that it was pretty clear that I would be transitioning to John Eckhart's church and soon. So, I did the most obvious thing next. I googled John Eckhart. I was ready to see who it was God wanted to use to develop me. I was actually excited. But in minutes, that excitement would morph into confusion because while Eckhart was known for training and activating people in their gifts, especially within the five-fold ministry gifts, his ministry was located in Chicago, which was over 700 miles away from my home just outside Atlanta. Why would God reveal to me this name when there was no way that Eckhart would be accessible to me at this time. One thing I knew was that my work was beginning in Atlanta, and now was not the time for a great move. So, I made the next logical move. I began to search for training near me that Eckhart may have facilitated. There was nothing applicable at the time. So there I was, stuck. I knew that God was releasing me from my current church, but I was confused about where I would go next. However, the Spirit of the Lord so clearly announced that my time was up and that I was to make my Pastor aware of that immediately.

I obeyed the dream, and I made my Pastor aware that the Lord was pushing me out. I was very honest in sharing that I had no idea where I was going next or even whether this was a permanent thing, but I knew I had to go. My Pastor gave me absolutely no pushback. He thanked me for my service, and he accepted my letter of separation with very few words of expression.

So I was free, released, clear, and without a covering, a trainer, a mentor, a guide. One part of the dream was done, but how did the

Eckhart part look? And when would it happen? Well, let me tell you. It pays to be obedient because within a week or two of my church separation, I accidently stumbled on the person I would come to know as "my Eckhart."

In an effort to bring in some additional income, I began teaching piano lessons through an agency that provided the clients and arranged the lessons. Out of the blue, the agency reached out to me concerning an older married couple who lived in the nearby McDonough area. I was one of the few instructors with the agency who resided on that side of town, so the agency felt the couple would be a perfect match for me. So I took the job.

After two lessons, the wife, Brenda Culpepper, suddenly revealed to me that I was not there to teach her piano lessons. On the contrary, I was there to be taught. She said to me, "I am an Apostolic Prophet teacher, and I train Prophets. I had a School of the Prophets in Connecticut for years. God instructed me to move to Atlanta because he would be sending me budding Prophets who would need to be activated and trained in this region, and you are to be the first." I began to cry. I could not believe this was happening. And then, after we had made our first scheduled training session, the Eckhart part of the dream became very clear. She handed me a book, and she told me to read it as a part of the class literature. Guess who was the author of the book? Yep. John Eckhart.

My life from that moment was completely changed. I had become knowledgeable about who I was. I had been activated. I had been trained. I had been changed, and within three years, I unexpectedly became Pastor Rachel through the working hands of Prophet Brenda Culpepper and under the covering of Dr. Iona Locke who was Prophet Brenda Culpepper's covering at the time.

But not everyone was celebrating my growth and development. Not everyone was accepting of it. Without my knowledge, Jezebel was already planning the attack to discredit all that God was doing in my life and in me. I would soon discover that the very dream that gave me the very instructions needed to bring me to this place of purpose in my life would also be the dream that would give a threatened and misguided Jezebel spirit a manipulative outlet to label me as title seeking, unaccountable, and wild. It would also be used to bring into question the legitimacy of my growth, my gifts, and the work of my ministry from the very church that initially showed no issue in releasing me to grow.

My motives were pure, and I didn't move out of the church on a self-seeking impulse; I moved because of the divine instruction of a Holy Spirit dream with absolutely no knowledge of what I would come into being. Yet, it would hurt my heart to discover that words like "pure" and "God" had been totally omitted from the picture, and the church leaders perceived my actions as something self-seeking and without godly direction, just as the leaders of the church had done to my father decades earlier. The proof of this would meet me at my ministry's door when someone who attended my previous church—someone who often visited with us during the week—abruptly stopped coming when he was suddenly confronted by his Pastor, my previous Pastor. The Pastor told him never to return to my ministry again because it was not legitimate and that I was accountable to no one. This was painful to even swallow. Was this really taking place? What had I done to be perceived and described in this way? This was wrong, and yet, it was all made to look and sound religiously justifiable. But what hurt the most was what it did to this visiting soul. He was devastated because it would end all the teaching and training he had so thoroughly come to love specifically when it came to the studies of dreams and dream interpretation. He too was a prophetic Dreamsmen, but the emergence of this gift would be cut short under the authority of an awakened and uneasy Jezebel spirit.

Nevertheless, I was beginning to come into the full knowledge of the Dreamsmen in me. My gift to see had been activated, and I was dreaming more than ever. I was dreaming literal dreams and symbolic dreams. I was dreaming about myself, but more often than not, I was dreaming about others. Some I knew such as family members, church members, former classmates, past acquaintances, and coworkers; some were famous people that I didn't know such as John Eckhart, Kanye West, Bill Cosby; others were people I had not met personally, but I recognized who they were afterward when the dream manifested itself. Many times, I dreamed about something very foreign and totally unfamiliar to me like the nation of Syria or a military invasion. I was seeing people from my past in situations that God would use me to interpret and share only to discover that what had been shown to me was exactly what they had been experiencing. My gift was sharpening, and so was the gift of interpretation. Many times, I was called upon to interpret the dreams of others, and I did. I learned to prepare myself to receive the dream of the Lord, and I found in this season of my life that God was stretching and teaching me to trust the gift inside of me with every obedient moment that I shared the dream, no matter how foreign the dream or how unfamiliar the person receiving the dream was to me. Finally, God would go on to trust me with the ultimate test—the dream I would not want to have. The dream I would not want to share. This was my Jonah moment in which I wanted to say, "God anything but that." But it was out of my control. I was an appointed Dreamsmen, not by choice, and I was given my orders. This time, it was the person to whom the dream applied that would rattle me.

I had a very vivid and descriptive dream concerning a pertinent wind of change that would hit my old place of worship. But the dream came with great insight and instructions as it showed why the wind of change was being allowed by God and what the Pastor(s) would need to know to come through it as God would have them. It was so very detailed that I knew it was to be shared with the Pastor. It was God's way of making sure that when this challenging wind came, if I had not already, it was not to burden them and it was not at all permanent, but it was God's way of getting their attention about something that needed to be addressed. Of course, I wasn't exactly this Pastor's favorite person, so wouldn't he question the legitimacy of God in this? Why would God do this to me now? Why couldn't I dream about anyone else? I felt like this was me just voluntarily walking into conflict where there didn't have to be any. Couldn't I just pray for them? But the answer was clear. I couldn't just retreat into prayer as an alternative because the whole point of the dream was to make the Pastors aware that the challenge would come, or to identify the challenge had it already come for what it was so that they could quickly recognize how to officially conquer it.

Like father, like daughter, except I was already expecting the worse. I wrote the dream out and emailed it to my former Pastors. For days I received no response and then finally the Pastor's wife who was also a Pastor apologized for the late response and let me know that *she* had thoroughly read through the message and what *her* intentions would be. It was very clear that the same could not be said from her husband who gave no form of acknowledgment at all. It was as if he had me blackballed from his mind, his heart, and his church. Because the same principle held true for the rest of his leadership. The two leaders I had mentioned earlier who refused to even hear the dreams that had been shown to me through a Holy Spirit–endowed gift were a part of his leadership team.

It was clear that a true gift had been made to look insignificant because people didn't agree with God's choice of gift distribution. How haughty can we be to choose to disregard without a second thought a primary method of communication by God because of what we *think* we already know? If we understood what the dream is to God, we wouldn't be so quick to put it aside. If we understood what kinds of paradigm shifts could be manifested because of a dream, we wouldn't be so quick to belittle it as something optional for us to hear. For every dream we chose to ignore, we put ourselves at greater risk of missing our assigned purpose in God and missing the will of God.

Both dreams revealed what God desired both of these leaders to be or become in the present state of their lives, and in one case, a strategy was revealed to achieve it. This strategy would have exponentially expanded the leader's business by leaps and bounds, which ultimately led to her traveling and taking speaking platforms that would equip and transition young women for change. This, I was never, ever to release, but to whose detriment was that?

Further along in my walk, I shared a dream with a prominent church leader that exposed some very dysfunctional behaviors hindering the ministry from going forward in the perfect will of God. It also provided direction to some of the changes that would need to be executed to ensure that what God wanted to see manifest, under the leadership of this leader, would manifest. After revealing the dream, the leader quickly acknowledged how closely the dream aligned with the vision that had already been given to him and that he was aware of some of the things hindering the ministry, but when it came to the changes that needed to be executed according to the dream, the leader's response was that nothing can stop the will of God even if those changes weren't made. In other words, it became clear that the leader had become comfortable with his system of operations, and nothing was going to push him to change it even though the dream was showing something different.

One of the reasons we stay a stuck and complacent people is that we are unwilling to access and use the gifts God brings our way. Dreams are a gift and a true commodity. Their value is priceless because you cannot price life. And that is what they bring. Dreams give instructions and guidance to obtain the abundant life that was promised through the death of Jesus Christ in every functioning godly system. When we unknowingly get too cardinal in our operations and start to stray away from the intended will of God, He will shake us up using His gifts to the body because He loves us and wants to see His perfect will executed through us.

Joseph was about to do something that seemed right to him in his cardinal mind. He was about to divorce Mary because he found out she was pregnant before he had even been with her. And here's the thing, a divorce would have been considered the most gracious and kindhearted act of love because Mary could have been disgraced and put to death justifiably. But by God's spiritual standards, a divorce could not have been further outside the will of God. In fact, the divorce would have turned Joseph completely against the will of God. So, it was with a dream that God instructed him to do the exact opposite so that the Savior of all mankind could be born. It was the dream that revealed to Joseph the very strategy that would keep Jesus the Messiah, the Savior, alive. Imagine that, Jesus's very birth was secured by Joseph's willingness to listen to the dream, and then to obey it. What if Joseph treated the dream as so many in the body of Christ do, especially leaders, when what the dream is instructing or showing goes completely against what we have identified as right.

Dreamsmen are Prophets, and they are meant to speak. If we can accept the Prophetic words from Prophets whose downloads are audio-based, we should be just as accepting of the Prophet who is seeing and hearing in their sleep. In fact, my preference *is* for God to speak to me through the dream as he narrates to me by the Spirit what I am seeing because while someone may question what I heard, it's hard to question what I saw with what I heard.

I truly believe that Dreamsmen are a mechanism God is using in the 21st century to shut the Jezebel down and bring all systems together to work according to God's perfect order. When the church is truly righteously established, it will have the influence to bring order to worldly systems (government, education, business, etc.) that will see the church as the center of all operations. If we can dispel Jezebel, people can become and then take their rightful places on the kingdom wall. Dreamsmen are not just dreaming about church; they are also dreaming of systems that will need the influence of the church or the maturely developed believer to operate in the world according to the will and purpose of God. Church isn't for the church. Church is for the world. And a Dreamsmen is a bridge that drives the church to its connected purpose in God to be the central headquarters of the world. Through the dream a whole redemption plan was able to be executed because someone followed the instruction that would allow the birth of Jesus Christ. Through the dream, an entire nation was able to stay fed and live through seven years of famine because somebody was able to adequately prepare. Whatever God is telling the church through the dream, we have got to listen because what God is trying to accomplish through the dream is by no means a small thing. It never has been, and it never will be. Jezebel hates Dreamsmen because the dream gives the secrets to overthrow any Jezebel-operated system whether it is purposely operated or not. Church, let's not be afraid to listen, and let's not make it hard for the Dreamsmen to do what they are purposed for. Dreamsmen, you have got to go to work in this land.

Me? Well, I chose to finish what my father could not, and whether the church accepts it, it is my duty as a Dreamsmen, as it is the duty of all Dreamsmen, to continue sharing the dream that will expose hidden chains and free hidden gifts.

# CHAPTER NINE

# A DREAMSMEN'S DREAM ORDERS AGAINST JEZEBEL

The most difficult thing about a Dreamsmen's dream is that it typically comes with orders that seem to disrupt the already existing "appearance" of order and is contradictory to anything we see naturally going on at the present time. A Dreamsmen's dream is not to keep things as they are but to help move things along to how they need to be according to the purpose and plans of God. Dreamsmen evoke change from what is. In other words, if God has sent a Dreamsmen with a dream or with an interpretation of a dream your way, there is something God needs to bring to your attention for his plans to fully manifest themselves in your ministry, in your church, or in your life. Somewhere, the threat of Jezebel is existing over your life.

Here's another hard truth. Ninety percent of the time, the Dreamsmen's dream is not revealing something that was already known, already seen, or already felt. The Dreamsmen's dream is sharing something you do not know, you did not see, or you did not catch because it remained hidden under the careful and watchful eye of Jezebel. The Dreamsmen's dream comes about when God has determined that something needs to be shared or revealed—something that for whatever reason, God cannot get you to see or believe on your own. This is where believers often drop the ball. The mistake we often make as believers is that if we didn't see it, if we didn't catch it, or if we saw no evidence of it and the meaning of the dream brings us discomfort, then we toss the dream aside. Why? Because we, as believers, Prophets, Pastors, and ministers are made to believe that God would have shown us something before it occurred or before it came through "you," a Dreamsmen. But we neglect to consider that maybe we have overlooked the very signs God has given us because we're under the influence of a Jezebel, or maybe, we have unknowingly become so self-absorbed in the "good work" that our spiritual channels have been intercepted, or just maybe, for whatever reason, this was just the way God chose to release the information. But what we, the body of Christ, must train ourselves to acknowledge is if God sent the dream, then he intends for His perfect will to come from the dream no matter how difficult the means of getting there.

Some years ago, a "believing" young man I casually knew by way of association used his social media platform to share a very vivid account of a detailed dream that left him a bit disturbed. He didn't understand the dream, but he had enough knowledge to know the dream was worthy of interpretation. He ended his dream post with this: "If anyone has the gift of interpretation, please reach out to me and tell me what this dream means. Thank you."

I was so relieved to see the request at the end of the post because as I was reading the dream, I was seeing in all clarity the meaning behind the dream. And because this dream was so intense in nature and intended to be a pivotal moment for new direction in his life, I actually desired to have the opportunity to share with him the full depth of this dream. This young man was a natural leader with heavy influence. He needed to hear this. I was just looking for the very open window he had just given, or should I say, the open window God had just given for him.

I immediately reached out, introduced myself with regards to my gift, and proceeded to ask him if he was okay with me sharing the meaning given to me by way of the Holy Spirit. Again, he gave me the green light. His dream was a full story. It was like a motion picture jam-packed with real action and sequential events. I can recall to this day his mention of a full police officer scene, his friends and followers being captured, a safe place that wasn't at all safe, him calling Jesus over and over again for help while being on the run, and him taking multiple gunshots to his body until he was shot down as he tried to understand why Jesus hadn't protected him. That is not the full version, but simply my way of giving you a glimpse into the dream that disturbed this young "believer."

The interpretation of this dream was not a good one. There was so much going on in the dream. Each scene was critical. The Spirit of the Lord used every scene for interpretation, which gave so much relevance to the dream's overall meaning. The breakdown was plain and simple. I said to him:

> What you are believing and teaching others is contrary to God's and Jesus's teachings. Whenever God has tried to correct you, you fire back without any understanding. You have been operating against God's authority and outside His law. Therefore, it has placed you and those you have influenced in a dangerous place. Yet you have made yourself believe that you are safe because you are doing what you are doing in Jesus's name, so you will not surrender. But this way, son, only leads to sudden death, and in your time of trouble, Jesus will not be found.

As I stated earlier, the interpretation itself was not at all a good one, but now that the interpretation had been given, the real focal point became what having the interpretation could do for the young man's life going forward. He was given a heavenly perspective on something he didn't quite get. Now, a light was shining in a darkness he had become immune and accustomed to. I thought, now, he can walk in God's truth.

But the opposite occurred. He became hostile. He shifted. His willingness to listen turned into a stubbornness to hear, and he begin to attack me and the validity of the interpretation. Ironically, he responded the same way he responded to the officer in the dream. He began to defend his knowledge of the "faith" and all of what he does to support it. Then he refused me any further access to communicate with him on that social media platform. I was dumbfounded. This young man admittedly acknowledged that he had no earthly idea of what his dream meant, but when the interpretation enforced an uncomfortable change from what had been, it became very easy for him to reject the interpretation of this Dreamsmen. God had sent the Dreamsmen to help bring this young man, this natural leader, to a new place in his life for God to truly shine, and the aggravated spirit of Jezebel rose up and had him perceive the interpretation of the dream as some form of judgment.

It is time the body accept that Dreamsmen are not God's method of punishment. Dreamsmen are not God's way of bringing shame to you or your house. Dreamsmen are not God's bad anything. Dreamsmen are the superheroes to the unsuspected active Jezebel villain operating so elusively in the body of Christ. In fact, the very release of a dream or the interpretation of a dream through a Dreamsmen is a gift from God and should be received as such. The dream saves, restores, frees, revives, corrects, and fulfills for us to break free of the strongholds of Jezebel and receive the very generous benefits of a life aligned to the perfect will of God.

Daniel's interpretation of Nebuchadnezzar's dream that he would lose his sanity wasn't to shame him. It wasn't to undermine him or show him up. It wasn't to strip him of his power or minimize his role as a king. It was to make sure he could continue to carry out his role as a king according to the way God had ordered it. It was to stop an action that Nebuchadnezzar saw no fault in. Why should we, the body of Christ, allow ourselves to be offended, upset, or hardened by the very thing meant to set us free?

Yes, the dream and its interpretation do come to expose and dispel, but it's not the believer or leader they are coming after. No. The dream and its interpretation are coming to expose and dispel the lie to which Jezebel has been holding the believer or leader hostage. Think about it. The body of Christ will never operate in its full power and authority if we are still bound in chains of deception, manipulation, pride, ego, intimidation, fear, and control especially when we are completely oblivious to it. Remember the Jezebel spirit has made its hiding place in the church. What makes us think we don't need another set of lenses to scoop her out? Why wouldn't we want another pair of lenses to scoop her out?

This is what Dreamsmen are. They are the amplified set of lenses pointing Jezebel out when it has become difficult for other leaders or believers in the body of Christ to see her. The key phrase is, "when it has become difficult." This means you are very likely to not at all have detected, seen, felt or sensed what it is that the Dreamsmen is revealing to you.

On one occasion I had a dream that a highly recognized and respected Bishop was trying to fondle me while his wife was lying in the bed right next to him. His attempts were immediately interrupted when my husband raised his head from beside the bed to say something. After my husband finished saying whatever it was he had to say, the Bishop kept his hands to himself out of fear that my husband would see and expose him. The dream transitioned to a room where the wife and I were engaged in a conversation. She then very boldly proceeded to tell me that she was very aware of her husband's shenanigans, but to honor his good name, she had been going along with them and keeping him covered. But this! This had put her at her wit's end and now she was publicly ending the marriage even at the expense of their ministry.

I did not have a relationship with this Bishop nor a method of communicating with him. I may have sat in a training here or there, but I did not know this man. The only thing I knew at this point was how real this dream was and that it would play an integral part in prevention.

I did not know this Bishop's lifestyle, his history, or anything else for that matter, but I knew if he let this struggle overtake him, it would mean the end of everything.

Again, I did not know him, nor was I in his circle, but I knew someone who was, and I knew this person could be trusted with this information. I mean this person was all I had as a means of communication to the Bishop anyway. So I shared the entire dream with this other leader in hopes that the dream would reach him. Surprisingly, this leader disclosed to me that while there was a huge scandal centered around this exact behavior in the past, the Bishop had truly learned his lesson. This leader then went on to say, "There is no possible way he would even think of doing that again. He knows he would lose everything, so I am a little lost at why God would show you that."

Did you see what just happened right there? This leader's confidence and assurance in the Bishop's faithfulness based on the present knowledge about his past and his present accomplishments would not allow this person to accept the fact that this dream was stating the exact opposite. My assignment, however, wasn't to convince this leader. I knew that, like the dream, if the Bishop knew that God had someone on his radar, it would make him think twice before engaging in this act once again. I felt that just the disclosure of this dream alone would save his life whether he was already thinking about it or coming into a situation that would bring the thought on. I knew what the present situation suggested, but the dream exposed a truth that once revealed would keep the Bishop in the place God needed him to be. Again, this was not to condemn the Bishop or to judge what appeared to be his area of weakness. Dreamsmen are not judges. They are messengers. And this message was to remind him that he was on God's watch and that he would still need to uphold God's standard of ministry.

On another occasion, my husband and I had a big disagreement. I cannot remember to this date what it was about, but I knew I was right. I had argued my point until I made him feel like he was foolish for not understanding or seeing things the way I had explained them. I had logic, reason, and just plain common sense on my side. He was wrong and he should have been made to feel bad to try to make me believe that I was wrong. By the time I had finished pushing my point, he had humbly and gently apologized. Finally, I got him to see. I won. But then, came the dream.

That same night, I had a dream. And it showed me things my husband would never say to me or maybe things he could not articulate to me that changed my whole perspective. I was so wrong, and God showed me why. Not only did God show me why I was wrong, he showed me how my ego or my pride in wanting to be right blinded me from seeing the hurt I was causing and the rift I was building in communication between us. This was unbelievable to me. Not only did I think I was right, I made my husband think I was right. I had gone to sleep knowing I had made my point, and I was feeling good only to have God show me how I had totally missed it.

The following morning, I woke up and I told my husband everything. I didn't hesitate. I didn't hold back parts to make me look good. I told him everything I had seen and what I had interpreted from it. He confirmed everything God had already shown me. I could see the relief and the gratefulness on his face for what God had done for him. Then I apologized. I admitted to my wrongs, and I sought his forgiveness and God's.

I couldn't see it my husband's way, but it did not make my husband wrong. I had it all worked out for me, but that was not working for God. It took a dream to expose this, and like that dream, God gives the church Dreamsmen to do the exact same thing. He simply wants His point of view to be heard and considered no matter how painful the reality, no matter how right we think we are, and no matter how well things are working out for us. It would be a beautiful thing to God if a Dreamsmen could walk in a church, address its leader(s), and say, "I had a dream that you were holding brother Jackson inside a cage. He needs to be released so that his gifts are free to operate." Ideally, the leader would respond with, "Wow, I had no idea. Lord, forgive me for what I have done. Show me how to release brother Jackson so that he is walking according to his purpose." And then, just like that, God's work would be done.

Imagine if a Dreamsmen approached the leaders of a church and said, "I had a dream that you were running an entertainment show in church to gain more money, and when what was pure walked in to speak truth, you silenced her because you were afraid it would interfere with the crowd that came for the entertainment." Again, ideally, the leaders would respond with, "Lord, forgive me. I will tear down everything I had going on that was not pleasing to You, and I will welcome Your truth into Your House." That would interrupt the enemy's plans entirely.

Jezebel would cringe if a Dreamsmen were able to approach the leaders of the church and say, "I had a dream that the church got turned around. Everybody you had in the front is now in the back, and everyone who once sat and operated in the back is now in the front. God said let the overlooked take their place on the front line." Then the leaders would respond, "Lord, not my will, but Your will be done. Help me to make the changes You want enforced on this day."

The examples above were real dreams that I had about real churches. Real dreams. Real churches. Unfortunately, those were not the real leadership responses because the body of Christ does not acknowledge the dream and the interpretative power of the Dreamsmen, and that is not by accident.

The body of Christ has completely gotten away from what the Bible has demonstrated to us time and time again. Wasn't it a dream that told Abimelech not to mess with Sarah? It appeared that Sarah was available; after all, Abraham was telling everyone that she was his sister. But to keep Abimelech's hands clean, God used a dream to show him what no one else was able to see. The body of Christ has to get back in a place of reverence for God's dream even when there are no signs or evidence of the dream at all.

In the dream cases above, the absence of evidence, signs, or trouble made it hard for the body of Christ to receive the dream. There are other cases, however, when a Dreamsmen's dream orders are to clarify something a person has been shifting back and forth about. The individual knows, but then she doesn't know. The individual thinks so, but then she doesn't think so. Still, the matter at hand is so tied to her purpose, God can't afford for the individual to spend any more time guessing, so He sends a Dreamsmen in her direction. I have been this Dreamsmen on countless occasions.

There was a young lady who had visited my ministry twice. She was a close friend of one of our ministerial leaders. I didn't know very much about her except that she had a desire to coach and teach people the practical ways of living as a disciple of Christ. I think we may have spoken over the phone twice in a two-year period, and then one night, God placed her in my dream.

In this dream, we were in my church fixing some things up. She was sitting at the front, and I was cleaning up around the building along with others. I was engaged in a conversation with her, but in the midst of us talking, several young boys kept walking into the building one at a time. They all appeared to be in their upper teens. They would walk by and hug her and start working around the building. As I watched them embrace her, I began to ask her why she hadn't started her program for young boys. I asked her what she was waiting for. She sat there lost for words because she couldn't believe that I had come out and asked her that. I took her silence to mean she needed me to give her an answer, and I told her not to be scared. I told her she already had everything she needed, and that my ministry would help her in any way we could particularly when it came to the arts. I woke up, and I knew there was a call I would have to make.

I made contact with the woman about three or four days later. I explained to her why I was calling and that I had to share this dream with her even though I didn't know the response I would get. She listened in silence as I shared the dream and then the interpretation, which was that the young boys were waiting for her to take the seat and start the program. "Everything else around you will fall into place if you just start the program," I said. "Everyone was working around you while you sat in the seat. Start the program."

Crazy thing was, I had never seen any indication that she desired to work with boys at all. Up until the dream, all I ever saw her do was push her book, her coaching business, and her singles initiatives. I was going out on a real limb here, and none of it was making sense, to me, that is. Everything made sense to her. She began to cry and tell me about a program she had created years ago that she tried to give to other men to execute for young boys because young boys were the center of her heart. She could not believe God was bringing this back and sharing it with me, nevertheless. She explained how she felt young boys needed men, so she kept trying to leave the work for a man to do, but God kept instilling in her that she would be the "mother's voice" that they needed to nurture them into wholeness. On this night, my sister in Christ received the clarity she needed to move in her godly purpose.

Dreams like this and the ones mentioned previously are the very reason that Jezebel hates Dreamsmen. Dreamsmen interrupt common systems and enforce godly ones, no matter how common. Dreamsmen interrupt good systems and enforce godly ones, no matter how good. The ability to accept a Dreamsmen's orders rests in how humble, how meek, and how hungry you are for God's way, because nine times out of 10, a Dreamsmen's dream or interpretation of a dream must be followed by an act of change.

# CHAPTER TEN

# UNDER THE INFLUENCE—
# WHEN DREAMS GO IGNORED

Her seven-month-old son was dead. His infant life was no more. This was more than she could bear. This couldn't be her reality. I could feel every bit of her pain. I felt every ounce of her guilt. She would not be able to live with this. I could hear her thoughts, "How can I tell my husband that I am the one who killed our son? Why didn't I stop? Why? God please bring him back!" As she held her dead seven-month-old son on the bathroom floor, over the bathtub filled with water, her horrific cries echoed all through the bathroom walls. Her son's body was soaked. His lifeless body heavy in her arms. She knew he wasn't waking up. She knew she would never hear him laugh or cry again, and she knew it was all because of her. It was because she made the choice to leave her seven-month-old son in the bathtub unattended while she took a call to minster to, help, and assist two young ladies to whom she had already given so much of herself.

Earlier, she got off the phone having accomplished nothing but the contribution of time, and it was then that she remembered that she had left her infant son in the bathtub unsupervised. She hadn't even taken the time to make sure someone was with him. She hadn't even checked to see if he was settled. She just took the call as she had always done when her mentee girls needed her. It was her ministry. This is what she was supposed to do, wasn't it?

As she hurried up the stairs, she was craving to hear a sound, a laugh, a cry, a splash, something that gave evidence of life, and the closer to the bathroom door she got, the louder the silence became. She opened the door to a sight that would choke the very essence of life within her. But, this was all a dream.

I woke up in so much anguish piled up and covered with pillows of relief. This was only a dream. What great news! But the dream was so real, every emotion was lived, and I was instantly aware that while it was just a dream for me, it could indeed be this mother's reality if she missed the instruction to lay the assignment down. Those young ladies were now out of season, and if she continued to give this assignment any more time, it would result in the loss of her baby boy. It was obvious that I would need to communicate this information to her as soon as possible, but not before I prayed against the manifestation of this horrifying dream.

The dream had been given. The woman received it and understood that she could give no more of her time to her mentees or the projects connected to them. She was thankful for the dream, but most of all thankful to have her son. Her children were everything to her.

A few weeks later, she received a call from one of her closest ministry buddies Pastor Shaw. Pastor Shaw was having an event at her church for the young people in the surrounding communities, and not only did she invite this mother, her friend, to bring her children out to be a part of the games, activities, food, and entertainment, she wanted to know if she could also bring some of her female mentees to be a part of the entertainment. The woman thought, "Well, I'm going to be there anyway with my kids. It's not like I'm going to have to put any extra time into coaching them to be there." So, she accepted and assured Pastor Shaw that she would try to get a couple of her mentees out there to sing. This, after all, couldn't be the dream. The set wasn't even the same.

What the woman was neglecting to acknowledge was the instruction to lay anything down that would connect her to these girls.

It was the day of the big community event. The mother packed up all her kids, including her seven-month-old son, along with a few mentees. There were a lot of people traveling, so they all traveled together in three separate cars, one behind the other. During the drive, the young female mentees traveling with the mother and her kids kept the mother very entertained with their conversations. In fact, the mother was so engulfed in the conversation, that when they arrived and began to exit the car, the conversation did not stop. Even the other female mentees jumped out of the other vehicles and joined in the conversation. As the mother stayed heavily tuned in to the captivating discussion, she kept a light eye on her kids, watching them with great excitement, jump out the car, and rush off to the spot where all the fun was happening. She looked back to ensure every window was up and pointed the key remote to ensure all doors were locked. The mother and her mentees casually lingered behind the children keeping themselves grossly absorbed in their own fun.

Upon entering the event gates, everyone became preoccupied in their own activities. Some were eating. Some were playing games, and others were just hanging around talking. At this point, everyone was doing what they could before the entertainment portion began, which would include a vocal performance from the female mentees. It was very hot outside. We're talking a 98-degree July day. Trees and shade were scarce, so the mother and everyone else traveling with her, knew that they could not be out there for too much longer.

About 40 minutes or so into the event, it was time for the performance. The girls got up and performed their set. The mother stood by with great joy watching her mentees do what they did very well. The day had gone well. No hiccups. No slipups. No issues. I mean, it was a pretty great day. Almost an hour had gone by. The Georgia heat had won and persuaded the mother to round up her troops to head out. Because they would be short one car, other traveling arrangements had to be made. While talking over the new car assignments, one of the mentees looked at the mother and said, "I would ride with you in your car, but you wouldn't have any extra room for me with all your kids." At that very moment, all the mother heard was "with all your kids." Her heart sank. Her stomach became queasy. Her reality just changed: "With all your kids" was the trigger. "With all your kids" was the reminder that she had not taken all her kids out of the car.

All this time they had been talking and laughing and hanging—and not once did she remember that she hadn't removed her infant son out of the car seat and out of the car. For almost one whole hour, her seven-month-old son had been sitting in a parked car, in 98-degree weather with every window rolled up and with no one to attend to him. This could not be happening. This was the dream being relived. Except now, this was real.

The mother cut the young lady off and blurted out, "I left my son in the car." The mentees closest to her took off running toward the car to see about the infant. The mother ran with them hoping and praying, just like in the dream to hear an infant's cry, an infant's scream—something to tell her that her son was alive. If this was the dream, then her worst reality would be realized in the next few seconds.

She ran out the gate. The car was now in plain sight, but she could hear no sounds. "God, please let me hear my baby. God, please let me hear my baby," she repeated while running hysterically down the road. And then it happened. She could hear the screeching cries of a scared, irritated, and tormented baby. At that moment, this was the greatest sound on earth. She had made it to the car. She unlocked the car, pulled her baby out. His skin was flushed. His body and clothes were soaked. He felt like he had come right out of a pool of water, but he was alive. The mother removed his clothes and began to cool him off with water retrieved by the girls. As she held her son and tended to his needs, she could do nothing but cry.

She remembered the dream. And she knew how this was supposed to end. Her son was supposed to be dead. Scientifically speaking, 15 minutes in that kind of heat should have taken him out, but he was alive. The very thing the dream told her not to do, she did, but by the grace of God, by His mercy, and by His powerful miraculous hand, He chose not to make it so. This woman would never ignore the instruction of a dream provided through a Dreamsmen again.

For those of you who have gotten to this part of the book and still refuse to accept dreams as a primary method of communication by God, know that your refusal does not come without a cost. You see, when a Jezebel spirit is in operation, she desires to keep you under her influence. The way you break from under the influence of a Jezebel is to come into the full knowledge of truth so that you are freely able to carry out the instructions God lays out for you to become. So, every time you reject the knowledge of God in any form or His truth, you have brought yourself under the influence of Jezebel.

God was trying to prepare this woman for the new thing he would be calling her up to, but she had to be willing to stop doing what she had become so accustomed to. This was difficult for her because it was a good work, but it was no longer the work God had chosen for her, thus transforming it from a good work to a hindering work that now stood in the way of God.

When under the influence of Jezebel, you may not know it, you may not feel it, but your path is compromised, and when you choose to stubbornly remain on the path of compromise, you subject yourself to spiritual deaths and abortions and the spiritual deaths and abortions of those connected to you. The baby in the dream did not just represent a natural baby. He represented the God-given assignments, dreams, plans, visions, ministries, and projects that we neglect or choose to leave behind and allow to wither away every time we allow ourselves to fall under the influence of Jezebel.

Allow me to explain what it means to be under the influence of Jezebel. The Bible says that Jezebel's body was devoured by dogs. All that was left was her skull, her hands, and her feet. This was not by coincidence. This was with intent. These parts were to remind us of everything a Jezebel is and everything a Jezebel spirit does. The skull represents the mind control Jezebel exerts over her subjects. The feet represent her ability to wickedly lead people outside godly paths, and the hands represent the ability to control and manipulate one's business, behavior, and gift with the goal and intention of stopping the work of God.

When you are under the influence of Jezebel, you are simply getting worked over by the enemy to ensure you never come into the fullness of what God has assigned to you and the fullness of what God wants to do through you. Whether it's by way of ego, flattery, deception, intimidation, fear, pride, praise, or recognition, if you are unable to stop, adjust, change, and drop at the direction of your God, you are walking under the influence of Jezebel. And this is usually discovered when that spirit of influence is challenged by God.

Jezebel isn't dumb. Jezebel knows how to play the church "hustle." Jezebel can successfully operate a church and thrive, just as she could successfully run her kingdom and thrive in her waking life. This does not mean, however, that her successful operations are producing God-ordained results. She has just mastered the art of keeping the body of Christ oblivious to what she doesn't want to be seen. So you see, it takes a very skilled opponent to fight against the manipulating influence of Jezebel. We need Dreamsmen to show us what we don't see and to point out the activities that we engage in knowingly or unknowingly that continue to fuel Jezebel's influence over our lives. We need to let the hero rise.

The body of Christ is paying heavily every day for choosing to remain under the controlling power of Jezebel. Leaders in the body are treating Dreams and Dreamsmen with pure instruction, insight, and revelation just as Joseph's brothers treated him simply because God showed Joseph what He didn't show them. In that story, while every attempt was made to bring Joseph down, Joseph still became what he was assigned to become, but in modern-day stories happening in the body today, the Jezebel spirit is tearing Dreamsmen apart, and some of them are retreating into hiding places never to fulfill the demands of their call.

What we don't see is how many lives they will no longer be able to lead out of bondage and the effect that will have on the lack of influence and lack of power in the church. What we don't see is how many leaders won't be pulled out of deceptive operations. What we don't see is how many people will die in the very schemes God wanted to see them free from, or they will die still full of everything they were supposed to be, and that blood is on our hands.

This affects everybody. We have got to slay the influence of Jezebel and prepare for the 21st-century influence of God's modern-day Dreamsmen. If we don't, the end result will be death. Something somewhere is dying every time we refuse to live as God has ordained it. We may not see it. We may not necessarily feel it, but there's a cost of death somewhere, and at some point, we will have to answer for our part in it. In the previous dream, the mother, though it was truly an accident, would still have been held accountable for the death of her baby. Leaders, Shepherds, and Pastors, though you may engage in hindering activities unknowingly, you will still be held accountable for the spiritual deaths of your sheep. Learn this lesson now from the mother. If it comes to you in Dream form by way of a Dreamsmen, listen and take heed. The church, or the body of Christ, is in a real state of emergency. If you do not believe me, maybe you will believe the dream coming in this next chapter. While its content is the epitome of all things creepy, its message is boldly unarguable.

# CHAPTER ELEVEN

# A MESSAGE TO THE CHURCH—
# LET THE DREAMSMEN IN

Here I was at what appeared to be a wake, but it wasn't a wake at all. A respected and beloved leader in the body of Christ had been dead for almost a year, but here his body was, lying flat on a table in the center of the room where church operations were carrying on. The believers, the members, the congregants were moving around in what looked like a funeral home disguised as a church, as if there was no dead body lying among them.

I showed up to the church for an evening service and walked into a congregation sitting in front of a dead body that reeked of the smell of a rotten corpse. They sat attentively listening to a sermon being delivered by the Pastor who was related to the corpse. Because of the Pastor's relationship with the dead leader and his leadership position as a Pastor, he had the influence with the people to make all of this seem fine and well. Not one person seemed to be disturbed by any of this. Upon seeing this, I immediately got freaked out and tried to walk away, but a few of the congregants made room for me to find a seat. Something was dangerously wrong here, but I sat and listened in.

Then as the Pastor continued to speak, the body raised up off the table they had so nicely prepared for it. I jumped back in my seat and speedily tried to make my way through the crowd to the door. But something suddenly stole my attention even from that. No one, including the Pastor, was shaken up. No one else was frightened. No one else ran. As a matter of fact, they began to hug on the corpse, help it up, and embrace its presence. They were happily talking with it and showing it around.

In a very creepy, zombie-like, and uncontrollable manner, the corpse began to move among the congregants, who welcomed him with open arms. The stench of death was spreading throughout the building, and no one was in the least bit bothered. I began to shout out, "He is dead. Can't you see he is dead?" Yet the people continued to eagerly interact with this walking, rotten-smelling corpse, dressed, by the way, in his Sunday best attire, which consisted of a dark beige suit. What was the matter with these people? This was no resurrection. This man was clearly still very much dead. He didn't even have the ability to speak anymore. Why was this difficult for others to perceive?

At one point someone tried to bring the corpse face-to-face with me, but I quickly dodged this encounter and ran in the opposite direction determined to get the heck out of there. All of a sudden, the congregants and their pastor began to migrate to another room to continue their fellowship over food. As I continued toward the exit, I was suddenly made very aware that I had not come into this place alone. My daughter Zoe had come with me. With this new knowledge, my priority to leave was overshadowed by an urgency to locate my daughter and get her out of there.

I turned back around on a mission to find my daughter. At that moment, the setting of the funeral home had somehow transitioned into what had been a very familiar place to me. I knew my way around. I knew where I was going. I knew where to find my daughter. By then, I had made my way from the door, through the foyer, past a sitting room, and into what I could only assume was a living room. At last,

I had reached my destination, but it wouldn't be gladness and relief that would overtake me. No, it was more like astonishment, anger, and desperation. Right before my very eyes was the corpse hovering over my daughter. Both its arms tightly wrapped around her, squeezing the very breath out of her, and making it almost impossible for her to escape out of its grip. My maternal instincts went into high gear. It didn't matter to me how it smelled, what it looked like, or how creepy the thought of touching it was. I dove over to the corpse, wrapped my arms around it, and with all my might, I began pulling it away. The whole time I was pulling, I was screaming, "Let my daughter go. Let my daughter go."

I managed to loosen the grip of the corpse long enough to give my daughter the opportunity to run out. She seized the opportunity. I then released the corpse from my grip, grabbed my daughter, and ran out of that place without a thought for looking back. This was the end of the dream.

While the dream itself may have been a bit scary, the interpretation of the dream and what it meant for the church or the body of Christ was a whole lot scarier, and it was all based on one very important symbol or character in the dream. She was Zoe, my daughter. And no, it wasn't about who she was, what she had done, her history, her background, or any of the above. It was her name and what her name meant. The name Zoe means "gift of life." Yes, that's right, "gift of life." Once I was able to identify through the Holy Spirit that that was my point of focus, the rest of the interpretation came flooding in.

The interpretation went as follows: An evil spirit has been released in the church or in the body to execute spiritual deaths. It seeks to accomplish this by making sure the people of God never tap into the gift of abundant life given to them through Christ Jesus. Its purpose is to keep the people of God from becoming who they were chosen to be. It is to keep the people of God from walking freely in their gifts. It is to keep the people of God trapped in bondage and held hostage. But that is not the worst part.

The worst part is that the church or the body of Christ has made this spirit feel welcome. They have embraced it. They prepared a place for it. They made it comfortable. They brought others over to meet it. They never once saw it for what it really was. Therefore, they never put up any fight against it or encouraged anyone else to stand and fight against it. With smiles, happy fellowship, routines, and services, the church—the body of Christ—has accepted death, and they did it cheerfully under the direction and guidance of their Pastoral leaders.

As a heavenly solution, God is preparing and sending a people who will see as God sees, and they will be able to identify this wicked spirit for what it truly is while exposing what it came to do. Sadly, this assignment will not go over easily, nor will it be done without a fight. And the reason behind this is simple. The church has been blinded and is operating heavily under the influence of this spirit. By the church's own invitation, this spirit has been given permission to maintain a controlling hold over them and is being fueled by the leaders' constant unwillingness to see because of the perks their relationship with this spirit has given them. With a leader's consent, this spirit is boldly squeezing the very life and breath of the Holy Spirit right out of the church. For this reason alone, breaking its grip will take more than a song and dance. It would take more than a great-sounding sermon or high-energy service. It will take more than the religious and traditional practices of church. God is going to need uniquely portioned seers, Prophets, and dreamers to bring to the light the real condition of the church. But these seers, Prophets, and dreamers need to be prepared to hold their stance against great "religious" opposition so that the people can finally be set free.

Therefore, my message to the body of Christ is simply this: let's not knowingly remain ignorant to the message of the Lord. The spirit represented in the dream above was the spirit of Jezebel. God wouldn't disclose this message if it wasn't a devastating truth plaguing the body of Christ. Up to now, our fight against her has been almost nonexistent because, up to now, the fight has been among ourselves.

The ammunition, the weapons, the cavalry that God has called and equipped to win this fight against Jezebel doesn't need a fight with you.

Dreamsmen are the 21st-century superheroes for the 21st-century attack of Jezebel. Spiritual deaths and abortions are hitting the body in a massive way. Too many saints are sitting around serving but not becoming, and their voluntary abortion is causing more voluntary deaths. This is captivity. Remember for every villain or captive situation that God has identified, He has prepared a superhero answer. The church cannot continue to fight against His answer. The church cannot continue to fight against the gifts of the Dreamsmen.

Leaders, Pastors, Ministers, and Apostles, it is time to do a self-examination. The Bible says in Matthew 24:24 that even the most elite could be deceived. Therefore, if you consider yourselves among the elite, then you should also know that this does not exempt you from operating under deception. It's time to self-reflect and ask yourself:

> Have I been visited by a Dreamsmen and disregarded the visit? Have I minimized, by my own arrogance, knowledge, or experience, the message or the instruction that was provided to me by way of a dream through a Dreamsmen? Have I allowed myself to be open to the correction or redirection sent to me by way of the dream? Have I flat out rejected the dream because it didn't make any sense to me? What example have I set for my sheep, my assignments, those connected to me about the importance of the dream?

Be real about your answers. Maybe in your honesty you will discover the Jezebel that was lurking about in *your* midst.

Leaders, it is also time that we begin to educate the body of Christ on the power of the Dream. While writing this book, my husband turned on the radio to hear a Pastor openly announcing over the airways that God no longer speaks through dreams. This was a leader, a leader with followers. So, what could this line of teaching do to a Dreamsmen's assignment? A Dreamsmen's ministry? How receptive will his members be should a Dreamsmen need to approach them with a message from a dream. How receptive will he be? Such a statement could not be any further from the truth. This is a true demonstration and wake-up call that it is time to execute and enforce the training that prepares the body of Christ to revere, respect, and receive again the power of God's dream. It's time to become a part of a Dreamsmen's upbringing and not a Dreamsmen's fall. Let us set an environment conducive to the healthy emergence of the Dreamsmen assigned to keep the body free of the influence of Jezebel. Let us all begin to take part in our own win.

Leaders, seek out the Dreamsmen with the understanding that a Dreamsmen's service under your authority does not make you less of the leader God assigned you to be. It amplifies you as a leader and keeps you in the place of accessing everything you need from God to carry out your leadership assignments to wholeness. If Jezebel's weakness is truth, then let us collectively work with the assigned Dreamsmen to push truth in Jezebel's face. Let's stop giving Jezebel cover. Allow the Dreamsmen to come on in and pull the covers off. This not only positions you and the body of Christ for greater works, but it enforces the rights of freedom given to everyone assigned to you so that captivity is not your church's portion. Let there be no blood on your hands.

I was reading a book written by Pastor Nancy Joy Dozier titled *Decree a Thing*.[3] There was a chapter in the book in which she spoke of a dream that provided insight about a person in her church body who, from the outside looking in, appeared to be a diligent servant to the ministry. Yet, this dream suggested the very opposite. The dream identified this same "diligent servant" as a demonic assignment sent to the church to cause both spiritual and physical death within the ministry. Because

---

3. Nancy Joy Dozier, *Decree a Thing: Creating Your World with Your Words* (Self-Published, 2019), 52.

of her respect, reverence, and spiritual education about the dream, she heeded it and placed herself on spiritual watch for this person. Within one or two days, she experienced the waking evidence of this dream. While carefully remaining on the spiritual lookout, Pastor Nancy was able to walk in and hear the demonic prayers this person was sending up inside the church, against the church. Without hesitation and because she was already on alert from the knowledge provided to her through the dream, Pastor Nancy was able to respond with a heavenly strategy to dispel that spirit back from which it came.

This is an amazing example of the victories the body of Christ could experience if they would humble themselves past their own level of knowledge and begin to acknowledge the message of the dream. The body of Christ needs Dreamsmen. They need their spiritual night eye, or night watch. Spiritual activity is highest between 12 a.m. and 6 a.m. Take note that Dreamsmen's watch is primarily taking place during these exact hours of the night. They are seeing what leaders and the body of Christ won't always see because spiritual activity is heightened during their watch. Additionally, they are literally *just* watching. While the body of Christ on their watch is in constant motion throughout the day fighting against flesh, bombarded by all the cares of life, distracted by "good" works, and blinded at times by their own desires, a Dreamsmen is simply *just* on watch. They can't miss it if they tried. There is no distraction. There is no work. Their desire at the time of their watch is irrelevant. When they are called by God to their night watch post, the Spirit of the Lord has the floor and has overridden any acting part of the flesh. Their information, their download, and what they begin to see come straight from the throne. What a powerful weapon to leverage with leading a body!

If the body of Christ truly desires to walk in the power and influence they are called by God to have in every mountain assignment, all over the land, we will need to prepare the church to receive the voice, the message, and the dream of the Dreamsmen. Leaders, churches, body of Christ, "Let the Dreamsmen in."

# CHAPTER TWELVE

# DREAMSMEN, YOU'RE UP!

Dreamsmen, it is my hope and prayer that the release of this book will play an instrumental part in making your assignment as Dreamsmen more acceptable in the land. But if it does not and stubborn hearts remain stubborn and tradition and religion continue to serve as a major point of opposition, do not let that stop you from being who you were called to be. You are not alone, and you can still win. Your assignment will still prevail as long as you are willing to take your stand. God will always back up a Dreamsmen, and those you have been assigned to share your dreams or interpretations with, whether immediately accepted or not, will come to know by the Spirit of God, and by the Power of God, that a true Dreamsmen was among them.

Please allow me to share one final dream with you. This is the dream I call the "T'Challa Dream" after the Marvel movie *Black Panther*. The movie opens with the famous scene in which T'Challa enters into the ancestral plain. He sees past kings in their animal form as panthers sitting in a tree. One of the kings is his father. In my dream, his father approaches T'Challa in human form and tells him,

"Your time as king has ended. It's time for you to take your place with us here on the ancestral plain." And similar to the scene in the movie, in my dream T'Challa fires back with:

> No. I have to fix what you and all the other kings before you have done. You have led wrong. I will not do things as you and the kings before you have done. I am going to make this right.

At this point the dream transitions, and T'Challa is standing in front of a large ocean body. In front of him is land filled with stubborn people staring at him in discomfort, anger, and doubt. They are whispering, chatting, and sharing opinions about their thoughts on what has been passed down to them concerning T'Challa's unwillingness to follow in his father's footsteps. T'Challa can hear it all, and he can see it all because he has the sharp sight of a panther, and despite what he is seeing, he is determined to bring about massive change. T'Challa puts on his mask and begins charging toward the land, and as he begins to charge, a huge tsunami-like wave rises behind him to give the power and the backing that he needs to bring change into the land. As the people see the water and the power T'Challa is moving in, they begin to give a different kind of attention to him and they start to take notice of what T'Challa is really capable of. The dream ends.

Dreamsmen, it is not your charge. It is not your duty. It is not your assignment to be what was. It is not your role or your purpose to go along with what has been. You have not been programmed to operate blindly. You have been given the spiritual eyes to see what you must to fix what was and align it with what God wants it to be. You are going to see what others won't see. You are going to know things that seem contrary to what others know. You, like the dream above, come to challenge the traditional and religious systems in the body of Christ that keep people from rising. You are going to challenge the traditional and religious systems of the body of Christ that keep the body of Christ from seeing. You are the Black Panther. You are the T'Challa in the dream, and you have what it takes to dismantle Jezebel.

The opposition will come. Jezebel will act out against you. She will try to discredit you. She will make every attempt to have you second-guess yourself. She will make false accusations about you. She will exert her influence on others and make you feel isolated and alone, but you are no more alone than Elijah was. There are still Dreamsmen out there ready to stand with you. There are still Obadiahs ready to vouch for you no matter how hard the dream is to swallow. Many will choose to ignore the dream, but you cannot. Many will not acknowledge the severity of the dream, but that is not a choice you can make. If all you are led to do is pray, then let that be the action that you take, but do not be afraid of your dreams because, in case no one told you, the dream is not your dream anyway. The dream is God's.

Furthermore, as a Dreamsmen or an emerging Dreamsmen, it is your charge to sharpen your gift as you help sharpen this gift in others. Educate yourself with all there is to know about the dream as you educate others. The more information you make available to the body of Christ, the better position the body of Christ will be in to receive the message of the dream.

Develop your gift through training and become very acquainted with the word of God. The more you know about God and His word, the sharper you will be as an interpreter of your dreams. The more you know about God, the better you will be at discerning a God-given dream. Fill yourself up with God's truth. Truth is Jezebel's weakness. It is difficult for a Jezebel spirit to fight against a Dreamsmen filled with the word of God and the Spirit of God. One thing you must not forget or disregard is that both Daniel and Joseph had very intimate relationships with God. A true Dreamsmen has to be in close relationship with God. A strong relationship with God will serve as a Dreamsmen's point of comfort when attacked by Jezebel.

Finally, as with Daniel, prayer must be a lifestyle for a Dreamsmen. A Dreamsmen's prayer will keep a Dreamsmen strong. It will run interferences for God in dreams that show devastating or unfavorable outcomes for the people of God, and it will serve as a strong spiritual point of extraction for a Dreamsmen's full interpretation of a dream.

Dreamsmen, it's time to gear up for the final combat. You have a Jezebel to break through. Now that you know what to expect, plan your strategy around Jezebel's. Now that you know who and what you are, do not allow yourself or your assignment to be diminished by Jezebel. The great thing about Jezebel's tactics is that they never change. It's the same battle plan every time. So be strong, get sharp, surround yourself with a spiritually educated support circle who understands and respects who you are and your power as a Dreamsmen and plan your strategy with God against hers. Elisha did, and Elisha became God's instrumental hand in bringing Jezebel to her death.

Dreamsmen, you have been summoned for the Final Combat against Jezebel. Be not dismayed; the victory against Jezebel is going to come through you.

# ABOUT THE AUTHOR

Rachel Senior is cofounder and Pastor of Kingdom Empowerment Center in McDonough, Georgia, alongside her husband Michael Senior. She is also founder of She Builds Women's Leadership Conference—a kingdom platform for building female leaders in business, the marketplace, and church. Rachel is also the founder of The Bethel Center, Inc. a nonprofit organization dedicated to the holistic development of the at-risk population of female youth. One of Rachel's recent achievements for the Kingdom is the establishment of Dream Talks, an educational platform, which includes dream workshops, dream training books and materials, and live media broadcasts designed for the 21st-century dreamer and the body of Christ preparing for the message of God through the dream. Rachel is mother to six remarkably talented children, and she loves every minute of being a parent.

# DREAM TALKS
## THE HIDDEN DIALECT TO PURPOSE

By the leading of the Holy Spirit, Rachel is sharing her gift of dreams and interpretation with the world through education and application. Rachel has recently launched Dream Talks, a platform for the 21st-century dreamer and for the body of Christ, preparing for the message of God through the dream.

Dream Talks is a compilation of dream training seminars and workshops, dream training books and materials, and a live media broadcast to raise awareness to the power of the dream. Dream Talks is designed to:

- Prepare the body of Christ to receive the message of the dream.
- Activate, train, and develop the dreamer of dreams or 21st-century Dreamsmen.
- Provide practical tools and knowledge to sharpen and advance accurate dream interpretation.

To inquire about my dream training seminars or workshops or to register for a seminar, visit www.rachelsenior.com or contact info@rachelsenior.com.

To enhance and activate the dream life of a Dreamsmen, visit my online store, The Dream Scene, at www.rachelsenior.com to order dream gifts and resources.

CPSIA information can be obtained
at www.ICGtesting.com
Printed in the USA
LVHW080002261120
672562LV00017B/334